CANADIENS CAPTAINS

Nine Great Montreal Canadiens

MICHAEL ULMER

Macmillan Canada
Toronto

Canadian Cataloguing in Publication Data

Ulmer, Michael, 1959–
    Canadiens captains: ten great Montreal Canadiens

Includes index.
ISBN 0–7715–7397–9

1. Montreal Canadiens (Hockey team)—Biography.
2. Montreal Canadiens (Hockey team)—History.
3. Hockey players—Quebec (Province)—Montreal—Biography.   I. Title.

GV848.5A1U55   1996   796.962'092   C96–930951–1

This book is available at special discounts for bulk purchases by your group or organization for sales promotions, premiums, fundraising, and seminars. For details, contact:
Macmillan Canada Special Sales Department
29 Birch Avenue, Toronto, Ontario M4V 1E2
Phone: 416-963-8830

Macmillan Canada wishes to thank the Canada Council, the Ontario Ministry of Culture and Communications and the Ontario Arts Council for supporting its publishing program.

Macmillan Canada
A Division of Canada Publishing Corporation
Toronto

1 2 3 4 5 FP 00 99 98 97 96

Printed in Canada

CONTENTS

To Cecilia Ulmer and Dina Bongers,
who made this book possible, and to Maddy,
who made it necessary.

ACKNOWLEDGEMENTS

This book was built on the memorable careers of nine very different men who represented the best of hockey's greatest franchise. I am not the first writer, nor will I be the last, to hitch his wagon to their greatness but there will be none more grateful to the players, their families and teammates. To Emile Bouchard, Maurice Richard, Jean Beliveau, Henri Richard, Yvan Cournoyer and Bob Gainey, thank you for being great. Also my thanks to incumbent captain Pierre Turgeon whose accomplishments may never rival his character, not because he is a bad player, but because he is such a good person.

The idea for *Canadiens Captains* came from Macmillan editor Kirsten Hanson, with the final diplomatic nudge supplied by editor-in-chief Karen O'Reilly. They are a formidable tandem, and each had faith that the captains of the Montreal Canadiens merited a book. Now, so do I.

Finally, to Doug Harvey, Jr., Dick Irvin, Frank Selke, Jr., Rip Riopelle, Bert Olmstead, Ken Reardon, Jean Roy, Herb Zurkowsky and the staff at the Hockey Hall of Fame, as well as the dozens of others whose help I depended on to write this book, my heartfelt thanks.

Michael Ulmer
Dundas, Ontario
May 25, 1996

NINE HANDS

The old man in the red jersey took the torch and walked out of the dressing room of the Montreal Canadiens, past the pack of camera people, technicians and assorted Dallas Stars, through the hallway, into the light. It was 10:20 p.m., March 11, 1996. Moments before, the Montreal Canadiens had beaten these same Dallas Stars 4–1 in their 3,221st and final appearance on the ice of the Montreal Forum.

In the room Emile Bouchard has just left, photographs of young faces, one for every Canadien in the Hockey Hall of Fame, line a wall. Above and below the cutouts, in English and in French, are the words from John McCrae's poem, "In Flanders Fields": "To you from failing hands we throw the torch. Be yours to hold it high."

The torch has long since become the central symbol of the Montreal Canadiens, that flame, the link that bonds the present with the glorious past. Bouchard, at 76 the oldest living captain, upheld the flame in his time by listening solemnly when a young man explained his money problems and by staring straight, unflinching, as his coach verbally abused him. Now he holds the torch out in his right hand, and a beefy left hand clasps it. Maurice Richard lifts the torch as he once lifted the province; steadily, pridefully, he walks across the carpet and hands it to the tall, silver-haired Jean Beliveau.

There are 19 Hall-of-Famers standing on these strips of carpet, scoring champions like Dickie Moore and Guy Lafleur, and goaltending great Ken Dryden, but only nine grasp the torch. This is an honor reserved for the captains of the Montreal Canadiens.

Henri Richard must reach up to take the torch from Beliveau, but reaching up to match the standard of bigger men is what landed "the Pocket Rocket" among the giants. A few moments later, Yvan Cournoyer breaks into a wide grin as he accepts the torch from Henri Richard. Speed as well as joy, beaming from that boyish face, was Cournoyer's calling card and while age has slowed his legs, it has yet to temper his smile.

On the procession goes, to Serge Savard and then to Bob Gainey, whose steady unerring gait defined him then and now, to the Dallas Stars' Guy Carbonneau, back in red for one night, and finally, to its current steward, Pierre Turgeon.

Unseen, but nonetheless remembered, are the hands of two more men. Doug Harvey coveted the torch, held it for a year and died a little when forced to give it back. As a coach, Toe Blake brandished the torch, and all it represented, always to demand more. Nine hands, nine men: Emile Bouchard, Maurice Richard, Jean Beliveau, Henri Richard, Yvan Cournoyer, Bob Gainey, Pierre Turgeon and, in this book, standing in for Carbonneau and Savard are Toe Blake and Doug Harvey.

Nine stories with common elements. Each man from a family of meagre to moderate means. All but Turgeon and Harvey enjoyed one spring day when, as captains, they were the first to clasp a newly earned Stanley Cup.

Nine stories for 22 captains, a string inaugurated with Newsy Lalonde in 1917. The captaincy was built, brick by brick, by the men who wore it, but not all have been giants. Walter Buswell, the club's eighth captain, left the Canadiens over a salary dispute in 1940 and never played again, while the tenures of Bill Coutu (1925–26) and Mike Keane (1994–95 to 1995–96) were memorable for their poor results and therefore their brevity.

Indeed, the captain's "C" has been both amulet and millstone. Jean Beliveau tried to give it back in 1961 and Chris Chelios and Guy Carbonneau factionalized the team when they shared it in 1989–90. Only time will reveal whether it will nudge Turgeon into the level of leadership craved by his patrons in the executive offices as well as his critics in the stands and along press row.

Many of the captains lead still. Beliveau turned down an offer to become Governor General of Canada to ensure he had time for his fatherless granddaughters. Cournoyer tutors young players every working day as an assistant coach with the Canadiens, and the remarkable Gainey thrives as the central pillar of his own family, as well as the general manager of the Dallas Stars.

If the C stands for character in Toronto, it signifies Champions in Montreal. The nine captains profiled here brought magnetism along with skill and purpose to their roles. One, Maurice Richard, came to symbolize passion, another, the

elegant Beliveau, grace. Harvey was outgoing and outra-
geous, Gainey wry and quiet, Cournoyer equal measures of
both. Each man led his own way. The greatest common
denominator, of course, was victory.

CHAPTER 1

TOE BLAKE

CAPTAIN 1941–1947

TOE BLAKE

CAPTAIN 1941–1947

J ohn Ferguson, a Montreal Canadien once more in the name of nostalgia, smiled at the thought of it: "Toe Blake would have loved this tonight," he said, shouting above the din of his fellow old-timers in the Canadiens' dressing room, March 10, 1996. Moments before, the oldtimers had beaten an NHL veterans squad in a prelude to the official closing of the Forum the next night. Somehow, Toe Blake, who had shaped so many of the lives in that room, first as a captain, then as a coach, should have been there, trading jokes, shaking hands, basking, as he always did, in the company of other athletes.

Students and apprentices of any sort often resent those who demand more, as Toe Blake did. For Ferguson, Jean-Guy Talbot, Yvan Cournoyer and many others, much of the best they had to give was summoned up in this room by Blake, and if the victories these men shared are uniformly rosy in hindsight, they were pitched struggles the first time through. Only experience matures our view, and often by the time we understand what has been done for us, it is too late for the taskmaster to be thanked. Toe Blake succumbed to Alzheimer's Disease on May 17, 1995. The men in the room must wait for another time to meet their mentor.

Toe Blake would be remembered as one of the most sterling captains in the Canadiens' history, but his success as a coach has almost completely overshadowed his image as a player. The sight of Blake behind the Canadiens' bench, fedora tilted back, is an enduring image of the old-time hockey coach.

Blake piloted what many consider the most talented group of players ever, the five editions of the Montreal Canadiens who won Stanley Cups from 1956 through to 1960. If Stanley Cups are the ultimate measure of greatness, Toe Blake was the finest coach in NHL history. His name graced the Cup 11 times: three times as a player (twice with the Canadiens and once with the Montreal Maroons) and eight times as a coach. Former Canadiens' coach Scotty Bowman is the only coach within shouting distance of Blake's eight Cups; Bowman won the Cup six times, including five times with Montreal. Among current NHL bench bosses, only Mike Keenan, Jacques Lemaire, Terry Crisp and most recently, Marc Crawford have managed once what Toe Blake did eight times.

"Toe was the ultimate coach," said Ferguson amidst the bedlam of the dressing room. "He had a memory like an elephant and he treated the players like men. He had a great feeling for the game and could mastermind behind the bench in a way nobody has ever been able to. Maybe Bowman can nowadays but Toe, Toe was just too smart."

And tough. As a player, Blake could be vicious with his fists and his stick, and he was so profane he was barred from the

Forum's billiards room for bad language. As a coach, when he sensed his players' concentration was beginning to wane, he threw things for effect and berated designated whipping boys like Ralph Backstrom, Floyd Curry or Ferguson relentlessly. But none of the combative elements of his personality convinced his players Blake didn't care for them. "Toe was like a father to me," said one-time Canadiens' goalie Gump Worsley. "I loved Toe," Ferguson said. "He was so good to me. He made my career."

Hector Blake was born August 12, 1912, in Victoria Mines, Ontario, just outside Sudbury, and grew up in the nearby town of Coniston. Hector was the oldest in a family that included seven boys: his parents, Wilmer and Arzelie Fillion, produced 15 children but four fell victim to disease and died in infancy. Wilmer worked at the Inco smelter and the Blakes endured crushing poverty. The 11 surviving children grew up in a four-room company house and their closets were nails in the wall.

Blake acquired his nickname when his infant sister Margaret pronounced his name in French. The second syllable of "Hec-tor" eventually became an anglicized "Toe."

The Blakes were raised to be athletic, and Wilmer often played on ball teams with four or five of his sons. Arzelie, who spoke no English, was tough and plain-spoken. Those features would be passed directly to their eldest child. "I really think Toe was a product of his upbringing," said Kenny Reardon, who played with him for five seasons and later paved the way for Blake's hiring by the Canadiens. "He came from mining country, he worked in the mines when he was younger and that showed through. He had a very dogged personality."

Blake played his first organized hockey in the Sudbury-Nickel Belt League in 1929. He graduated to junior hockey in Sudbury and played for the Hamilton Tigers, a senior team, for most of the next three seasons.

Blake made the NHL's Montreal Maroons in time for the Stanley Cup–winning year of 1935, but his statistics—no goals over two years and nine games—were wholly unspectacular. A few months after winning the title, he was sent down to the American League's Providence Reds. The Canadiens, however, were more impressed than the Maroons (both Montreal teams operated from the Forum), and traded goalie Lorne Chabot for Blake and center Bill Miller in February of 1936.

The idea of playing for the Canadiens entranced Blake, who found himself a teammate of his boyhood idol, the great Howie Morenz. "I was about ten years younger than Howie Morenz and I played for the Canadiens in 1937, his final year, the year he died," Blake once told a newspaperman. "But, hell, he was my hero all right. When I was growing up in Northern Ontario, I used to call myself Howie."

Blake, even at 23, could not skate with the 35-year-old Morenz, but seasoned by his stints in the minors and senior hockey, he acquitted himself marvelously against some of the toughest players in the league. It was his toughness, his absolute unwillingness to lose, whether in cards, pool, baseball or hockey, that defined Blake, first as a player and later as a coach. "God-damn right he was tough, he had fingers like hot dogs," said Reardon. "One time he took on the whole Detroit team. They all came after him and he stood there at center ice swinging his stick, saying 'Which one of you bastards wants it first?' It was like a bunch of dogs trying to get at him."

Another time, Blake and Reardon were drinking in Jack Sharkey's pub in Boston. Blake got into an argument over the amount of change he should have received from a bartender and Sharkey, a former heavyweight champion, stepped out from the back room. Sharkey, then in his late forties, backed his bartender and Blake said he was willing to fight him on the spot. Patrons and staff interceded and Reardon led Blake away. "That was Toe Blake," said Reardon. "He would be willing to fight the heavyweight champion of the world if he thought he was right."

In 1940, Blake was elected captain of the club, replacing Walter Buswell, who retired at 33 when the Canadiens would not grant him the extra $500 he was seeking in salary. Blake was the perfect choice. Not only was he fiercely opposed to losing, he often displayed a kindness toward struggling young players that they never forgot. "When I was there, Toe was considered the old man of the team," said Elmer Lach, his center on the Punch Line. "When you were a young guy, just feeling your way around, he and Bill Durnan would take you over." Players like Busher Jackson, who struck out in a trial with the Canadiens before finding stardom with the Maple Leafs, would never forget Blake's help.

As captain, Blake garnered respect largely because he rationed his own. While sympathetic toward younger players, his approval was hard won. "He was a very difficult guy to get to know," remembered Lach, "but once you broke through, you realized he was the cream of the earth. It just took him a long time to decide whether you were the right kind of person."

Blake's captaincy was one of the few bright lights in what was a lacklustre era in the club's history. The Canadiens were in the middle of a 14-year Cup drought when Blake arrived and he did not win his first Cup until the 1943–44 season, his ninth with the Canadiens. Blake capped a four-game sweep of Chicago with an overtime goal and that Cup represented the flowering of the Punch Line. The unit, Maurice Richard on the right side, with Blake on the left and Elmer Lach in the middle, scored all five goals in the 5–4 Game Four victory and accounted for ten of the Canadiens' 16 goals in the series. Blake led the final in scoring with three goals and five assists.

The Punch Line was the perfect melding of three very disparate talents. Richard, naturally enough, was the line's triggerman while Blake operated as a top-flight spademan along the boards and in the crease. Lach, a splendid playmaker, orchestrated the line from center and Blake's physical presence made mauling the Rocket, a dubious idea to begin with, absolutely ridiculous.

The unit peaked in 1944–45, the season Richard hit the 50-goal mark. Lach, Richard and Blake finished one, two and three in the scoring race and even at that, the Punch Line's dynamic style of creating offense was so overpowering, many were left wondering how they could fritter away so many chances. "The year Rocket scored 50 (1944–45), Toe should have scored 60," said Lach "They'd put two men on Rocket and that always left Blake open. But Toe was a hell of a player. He played hard, he was never fooled. He had a lot of imagination, which you have to have and which I think is missing today."

Blake played 13 seasons for the Habs and won the Hart and Art Ross Trophies in 1939 and, despite 50 penalty minutes, the Lady Byng Trophy for gentlemanly play in 1946. In

578 regular season games, he scored 235 goals and added 292 assists for 527 points. He was good for 25 goals and 62 points in 57 playoff games. He was a first-team all-star three times, a second-team all-star twice and he scored the Stanley Cup winning goals for the 1944 and 1946 champions. Blake's 1944 playoff average of two points a game (seven goals and 18 points in nine games) stood as the highest-ever total for 39 years, until Wayne Gretzky averaged 2.35 points per playoff game in 1983.

All of this would later get Blake into the Hockey Hall of Fame but it did not make him a celebrity in his hometown. Blake liked to tell the story of going back to Coniston by train in the summer of 1944. No one was there to greet him so he lugged his suitcase to the back of the station. "Hello Toe," said an old man with whom he had worked in the mines. "You leaving town?"

Toe Blake's playing career ended when he was 35, as a result of a badly broken leg he suffered in January of 1947, when he was tripped and slid feet first into the end boards at the Forum. When the Canadiens, impressed by Blake's leadership during his playing days, offered to let him stay in the organization as a coach, he jumped at the chance. Blake had no real business interests and no career plans outside of hockey and the transition from player to coach was a natural one. He had neither the qualifications nor the expertise to change fields and if anything, age had only increased his need to compete. Nothing could replace playing, but coaching at least kept him in the business and put food on the table.

Blake was sent to Houston, Texas, to coach Montreal's minor league team in the Canadian-American League and he led the club to a championship in 1948, his first year behind the bench. The following season, he was promoted to the Canadiens' Buffalo American League affiliate, but in Buffalo Blake found he couldn't coexist with the team's general manager, and he quit to take a job with Valleyfield of the Quebec Senior Hockey League.

The Valleyfield job afforded Blake enormous control in everything from player personnel decisions to arena bookings. A six-team league offered only 120 NHL jobs and accommodated only a fraction of the pool of players available, so while the league was not on par with the NHL, the caliber of play was still better than that of the American Hockey League. The only downside to the move was the departure from the Canadiens organization and Blake, ever the competitor, worked hard to make his longtime employer a lasting enemy. He delighted in thumbing his nose at the Canadiens' management and was anything but deferential in negotiations whenever his team was involved in a playoff series at the Forum.

In 1955, however, two factors brought Blake back into the Canadiens' fold. Dick Irvin's treatment of Maurice Richard had culminated in the Richard Riot and prompted general manager Frank Selke to demand his coach's resignation. Naturally, the ability to handle the incendiary Richard was an important element of the new coach's job description, and what better choice could there be than Blake, Richard's former teammate and mentor?

By this time, Blake's old teammate, Ken Reardon, had moved from the ice to the front office as the club's assistant general manager. Reardon, the son-in-law of Canadiens' owner Senator Donat Raymond, proposed that the club hire Blake. The idea drew an immediate negative response from general manager Frank Selke, but the ultimate decision lay with Senator Raymond. Reardon won his old friend the job with some peculiar hockey logic. "I told Senator Raymond and Mr. Selke, if you hate him so much when he's not on your team, imagine how you'll feel about him when he is," remembered Reardon. Reardon then sat down with Blake to develop a strategy for dealing with Selke. "I said, 'Look Toe, I know you're used to being number one and that's fine, but this is business and the general manager makes the decisions. If he expects you to play a guy because he's got someone interested in him, you play him.'"

Blake justified Reardon's faith with a Stanley Cup victory over Detroit in his rookie season. "The toughest one was the first one," Blake would say later. "I was a new coach. Detroit had won in the two previous years. Now, everybody is saying, 'Let's see you stop them.' The first game was at Montreal and they're leading us 4–2 going into the third period. Between periods, I put together a makeshift line of Jackie Leclair, Claude Provost and Floyd Curry. They got three of the four goals we scored in the third period. We won the game 6–4. I always think if we'd lost that game, everything might have turned out differently."

That Cup victory was just the first of the run of five Cups Blake would reel off in his first five seasons in Montreal. The Canadiens boasted a marvelous team, built around Maurice Richard, who enjoyed some of his most memorable playoffs under Blake. Jacques Plante was on hand to tend goal and Doug Harvey, the premier defenseman of his era, anchored the blue line corps. Jean Beliveau had broken through to win the scoring championship in 1953–54 and establish himself as the franchise's next great star and preeminent on-ice leader. But the ringmaster was Blake. While clearly knowledgeable, he eschewed spending a lot of time teaching; what Blake knew about was playing with desire and desperation. "Get mad," he would sometimes bellow in the dressing room when the Canadiens struggled against a weak opponent. "You're better than they are."

Dickie Moore remembers speaking to Blake in the 1955–56 season when Moore, then 24, was struggling to stick as an NHL player. Moore had great ability but knee injuries had hampered his productivity and sapped his confidence. He did not know whether Blake would scold him or coddle him. Blake did neither, but Moore came away with exactly what he needed. "Toe Blake told me, 'Just play your game. I can't teach you anything, you've already got it.'"

Blake was successful because he felt no need to impose a rigid system on what was clearly a spectacularly talented team. "Hockey is a very simple game," he would say, holding up his arms. "It's played in two Vs—one moving away from our net and the other moving toward theirs."

Coaching the Canadiens had a built-in advantage: by league statute, Montreal had the first pick of any Quebec player. But if it's true that Blake won with the best, it is also true he won because he made them the best. Blake's Canadiens played with a fluid, entertaining style that maximized the team's obvious assets. It was Blake who recognized Doug Harvey's ability to dominate a game and eventually permitted his forwards to hang high in their zone for lightning-fast counterattacks. He used a deep defensive center to key the transition game and eliminate odd-man situations on defense. Blake insisted his players had to be constantly in motion, and Harvey's penchant for passing only to a man who was already moving meant the Canadiens played what came to be known as the European style decades before the Soviets popularized it.

Like the best coaches, Blake had a total recall of personnel and situations. If a Canadiens' center had trouble winning face-offs against a particular opponent, Blake never failed to make the necessary adjustment. Losing a face-off in the Montreal end during a penalty kill was a grievous and long-remembered offense.

Blake understood a player's sense of pride. He made it a point never to embarrass a Canadien in front of the fans or media. On the bench, he did not look at players who had displeased him, instead, he delivered his instructions while staring at the game clock. Players were forbidden to carry their own suitcase in hotels. "When you play for the Montreal Canadiens," he would tell them, "you go first class."

As a player, Blake had initially rebelled against Dick Irvin's demanding and often caustic style, but it was Irvin who would become Blake's greatest coaching influence. "I always thought he took the best points Dick Irvin had, the emphasis on weight, the training, the discipline, tempered them and threw in his own philosophies and experiences," Reardon said. "Toe Blake was not a carbon copy of Dick Irvin but certainly a heck of lot of Irvin was in Toe Blake."

Behind every pep talk, every encouragement and admonishment was an almost obsessive fear of losing. Defeat enraged Blake who waged a career-long battle with his temper behind the bench. Once, after a period in which the Canadiens had played poorly, he entered the dressing room, destroyed a medical cabinet with a stick and left without saying a word. The worst incident occurred in Game Three of the 1961 final between Chicago and Montreal. Referee Dalton McArthur called a borderline penalty on Dickie Moore in the third overtime. McArthur had penalized the Hawks earlier in the overtime but when Chicago scored, Blake became so incensed he punched McArthur. League president Clarence Campbell imposed a $2,000 fine, which amounted to a heavy penalty since Blake's salary was $18,000. During the ensuing flap over her husband's attack on McArthur, Betty Blake remained blithely loyal. "Toe didn't do it for himself, he did it for the players who were robbed," she told reporters. "Besides, if he hadn't done it, I would have done it myself."

Betty Blake was the unseen hand in her husband's life. She was the daughter of a Winona, Ontario, fruit dealer, and Blake had met her during his time in Hamilton. They had three children, Joan, Bruce and Mary-Jane, who were raised virtually single-handedly by Betty. It was she who had to discipline the children, a task her husband deplored. It also fell to Betty to talk her husband down after a loss. "After a loss, he'd talk to my mom for hours," said Joan McDonald, the couple's oldest child. "I can't tell you how many times I would go to sleep to the sound of my mom and dad talking way into the night." On the rare occasions when he wasn't involved with the Canadiens, Toe Blake was thinking about them and the atmosphere in the Blake household depended on how the Canadiens had done the night before.

Given this environment, Joan encountered an unexpected set of obstacles in preparation for her wedding in May of 1958. "My dad didn't want to be bothered by any of the wedding details," said McDonald. "He wouldn't even get fitted for a tuxedo because the Canadiens were in the playoffs. But we had to know whether he was inviting members of the team. If the Canadiens won the Cup, it was going to be a big wedding. If they lost, none of them were going to be invited." The Canadiens defeated Boston in six games in the final and after a flurry of last-minute details, the entire team was invited. Joan Blake's wedding went off without a hitch.

Success often blunts the hunger for more but Blake viewed complacency as his most virulent enemy. He constantly looked for ways to keep his players on edge. Once a player offered him a cigar in recognition of a new baby. "Great," said Blake, accepting the gift, "now maybe you'll get off your ass and play some real hockey." Blake applied the same obsessive vigilance to his own life. To keep the pressure on himself, he signed a series of one-year contracts.

Like Irvin, Blake was fervent in his belief in the value of team over individual. "Toe always believed that as the team went, everybody went," said long-time Canadiens' goalie Charlie Hodge. "He always preached that. His speeches were continually about team, not individuals."

Reardon recalls a dispute with an airline representative when, because the airline oversold their allotted seats, one member of the club was asked to take a later flight on a non-game day. "I said, I don't mind, getting there an hour later," Reardon remembered. "So this person says, 'What's your decision Mr. Reardon?' Toe Blake says: 'His decision is if we all don't go, we are getting off. Kick one other passenger off or 18 of us get off. When we travel, we travel together.'" A volunteer unaffiliated with the Canadiens was found and a symbolic measure of team unity was preserved.

"I played for Toe for 13 years and there is no doubt, he had the greatest ability to get the most out of his players that I have ever seen," Jean Beliveau said. "I remember his first meeting in 1955, he looked around the room and said 'I've got some great hockey players here. But unless we play as a team, it won't matter.' That's how he coached, we played as a team because he never asked a player to do something the player wasn't able to do."

After a three-year retooling period, Blake had the Canadiens back in the winner's circle in 1965, and he took home his tenth and 11th championships in 1966 and 1968. But by then, change was everywhere. The league had doubled in size to 12 teams. Marginal players were now bona fide NHLers and the feudal power coaches and general managers had traditionally enjoyed was being eroded by player agents. Now in his late fifties, Blake felt suddenly out of step with the new era. "Maybe I'm wrong," he said at the time, "but it seems to me the players have this attitude that, 'If I don't play for your team, I'll play for somebody else.' It's not quite as hard to make a team as it was before, when we had six teams. That's natural. But this attitude . . . well, some of the players have changed."

The game's direction troubled Blake profoundly and the multiplying demands of the media, a largely manageable chore during most of Blake's tenure, made the job even more difficult. "If all I had to do was coach, I wouldn't have minded it at all," he once said. "Generally speaking, I enjoyed coaching. I enjoyed playing more but what really bothered me about coaching was doing all of the other things associated with the job. Talking to about 20 newspapermen every day. Being nice to some guy who came 300 miles to see a hockey game and getting him tickets. It's something I had to do, I didn't like it but I had to do it."

Blake never changed the demands he put on himself or his players as he grew older. But the NHL was taking its first steps from sport to entertainment, and the dilution of talent also meant a dilution of the values that governed Blake's working career. It was still important to win, but bloated schedules meant winning every night wasn't as essential as it had been. Weaker opposition prompted players to fall into bad habits that could be telling against good teams. Dates against also rans only meant greater embarrassment should Montreal lose. There seemed to be so much more to worry about. "Winning," said Gump Worsley, "meant one less evening staying up trying to figure out why we lost. You looked at him [Blake] and knew he pounded the pavement a lot of nights." "I remember, when I was coaching the Oakland Seals," said Bert Olmstead, "we had a little visit and he said, 'Jesus Bertie, things aren't the same.' He didn't talk very much, you had to read a lot between the lines with Toe. He was made of granite, and he didn't bend, and eventually, Toe's methods were wrong with modern-day athletes. That was hard on Toe. Coaching was his whole life."

Reporters could understand Blake's frustration. What puzzled them were the patterns of elation and despondency. During the 1968 season, Blake began to seem discouraged after what should have been satisfying wins and uncharacteristically placid in the face of frustrating performances. What nobody knew is that Betty Blake had breast cancer and Blake's moods depended primarily on how his wife was coping with treatments that day.

After the Canadiens won the title in 1968, Blake walked out of the Forum as the club's coach for the last time. He was 59. Change and his wife's illness had doused what had always been a rampaging need to win. It was time to go.

Betty Blake battled her cancer for another five years and even when her death became imminent, her husband could not accept it. "A lot of men of that generation did not like to face things," recalled Joan McDonald. "He was that macho type, he never would discuss her sickness and sometimes, he would just disappear. I had to go sit with Mom because he just could not accept the fact that she was leaving him."

Betty Blake died in 1973. Her death was the greatest sadness of Toe Blake's life. "After Mom died, Dad was lost," recalled Joan McDonald. "He spent a lot of time walking around the house by himself."

Blake never remarried or even considered it. His children were grown, but in spite of his retirement five years earlier, he still had his surrogate family, the Montreal Canadiens, and a place of lasting honor inside the Forum. He continued to draw a salary from the club throughout his life and the Canadiens paid for a car to take him to and from the rink.

In the late 1980s, friends began noticing Blake's growing difficulty in remembering names and anecdotes that he had once delivered rapid-fire. "It used to frustrate him," said Beliveau. "He'd get mad at us for not knowing the names and he'd get mad at himself too." Toe Blake was diagnosed with Alzheimer's Disease, but even in his decline, the Canadiens existed as a second family. As Blake's health declined, Canadiens' executive Floyd Curry spent countless hours caring for him. When the time came to put him in a nursing home, Beliveau, then a Canadiens' vice-president, huddled with the family to make the decision.

In his final years, Blake could not communicate and he dozed in his wheelchair. "What could you do?" Beliveau said. "He could not recognize you. You would just stand there for a few minutes, with no reaction."

He died in silence, May 17, 1995, "But if you want to be truthful about it," said longtime newspaper friend, Red Fisher, who covered Blake and the Canadiens from the 1950s, "Toe Blake died six years ago."

Apart from the couple of years when he coached Valleyfield, Blake was employed by the Canadiens from the day he signed, February 27, 1936, to his death.

Eulogies poured in, but the most fitting one was delivered by Blake himself before the Alzheimer's locked him inside his body: "Hockey has been my life," he said. "I never had the opportunity of getting one of those million-dollar contracts, but hockey was worth more than a million to me in plenty of ways."

CHAPTER 2

BUTCH BOUCHARD

CAPTAIN 1948–1956

CHAPTER 2

BUTCH BOUCHARD

CAPTAIN 1948–1956

It's a dreary morning in West Florida, one of a series of bleak days that marred a once-promising spring. The Patriarch, speaking from his home in Bellaire, has all the time in the world. "My wife, Marie Claire, has gone shopping," Emile "Butch" Bouchard said with a laugh. "So I can talk freely."

Bellaire, population 10,000 or so, is a three-wood away from Clearwater and has been Emile and Marie Claire Bouchard's winter home for 13 years. They are there for Emile's health: Bouchard has undergone heart surgery to tend to three blockages and the cold of a Canadian winter exacerbates his medical condition. Strict and visible law enforcement is a priority in Bellaire and the Bouchards feel safe and welcome.

At 76, the man on the other end of the line is warm and funny, gifted with both the candor of the old and the recall of the young. During the closing of the Montreal Forum he proved himself to be eager in mind and still superbly strong in body. He plays golf most days in Clearwater, where the starter, a former Detroiter who booed the Canadiens at the Olympia, now arranges premium tee times for his one-time nemesis. The letter-carrier is a fan and sometimes stops to talk hockey but mostly, Butch Bouchard is just one of a throng of expatriate Canadians who cluster along the Gulf shore waiting for winter to leave the North so they can go back home.

It is a tranquil life and no one has journeyed further to live in warmth and comfort than Emile Bouchard. Born in a tiny, rented house behind the Catholic church on Boyer Street in North Montreal, Bouchard was five when his family moved to a third-floor apartment in the city's east end. No matter what the address, Bouchard, his three siblings and his parents managed, albeit barely, to keep food on the table.

"From 1929 until the war, we were in the Depression, there was not too much money or too many jobs," he said. "We had enough to eat. There was the St. Vincent de Paul, which helped families who didn't have too much. My dad worked for the CPR in the winter, painting passenger trains and in the summer, he collected *chaumage* (unemployment insurance)."

Emile inherited a quiet nature from his father, Calixte, and a love of people and humor from his mother, Regina, an expatriate American from New England.

The youngest of the children, Bouchard became a provider at a very early age. He was barely 12 when he began growing vegetables for his family in a vacant lot near his home. He would sell any leftover produce door to door; a good basket of carrots could, after all, fetch 15 cents. The proceeds went back to the family. That sense of responsibility toward others would later be evident in his roles of husband, parent and teammate. Bouchard has a Spartan work ethic.

The family had no money to buy skates, so Emile went without them until he was 16. To participate in pickup games at nearby outdoor rinks, he would save his pennies and rent the skates from other children for five cents a night. On the many nights he had no money to pay, he played goal wearing boots.

In 1937, he graduated to Le Plateau secondary school and, using $35 borrowed from his brother Marcel, finally bought equipment: skates, pants, shoulder pads and gloves. It cost what for him was a small fortune, but at least now he could compete.

Playing defense meant his lack of speed would be less noticeable and his strength, built through daily calisthenics and push-ups in his living room, made him a force to be reckoned with, as he easily cleared opponents from around his crease.

Bouchard was one of hockey's earliest converts to the benefits of weight-lifting. "My father had a shed where he kept the wood and the coal," he said. "What I had for weight-lifting were pieces of railroad tracks. On the ties, they put steel plates and on the steel plates, they put the railroad tracks. As I went along, I added plates with baling wire. It was as good as I could have done in those days."

A friend of his brother was a government employee who spent his days inspecting beekeeping sites throughout the province and Bouchard, alert to the possibilities of extra income, decided to go into the honey business while still in his mid-teens.

Ownership of the apiary would keep Bouchard out of the armed services during the Second World War. "It grew to a point where I was making 100,000 pounds of honey a year so the government gave me a dispensation," Bouchard remembered. "I was a farmer and I couldn't be replaced by anybody."

Through the summers, Bouchard tended to his bees and sold the honey. In the winter, he continued his hockey, playing junior for the Verdun Maple Leafs, intermediate as well as high school hockey. All told, he played what, at the time, was an astounding 42 organized games in one year, and except for the Verdun games, all his hockey was played outdoors.

It was during this era that Bouchard earned his nickname. After a game spent tossing opposing forwards aside like bowling pins, Verdun teammate Bob Fillion dubbed the big defenseman "Butch."

To the teenaged Emile Bouchard, the Montreal Canadiens, seemed too remote even as a dream. But when he excelled in senior hockey, first in Verdun and then later with the Senior Canadiens, it became clear that Bouchard was NHL material.

"I never really thought about playing for the Canadiens, the idea sort of generated itself," remembered Bouchard. "When my senior hockey coach asked me to play at the Forum, it was the first time I had seen it. I had never seen a professional hockey game there."

In 1941, after two years of senior hockey, Bouchard, then 20, was signed by the Canadiens. He spent six weeks with Providence of the American League at the end of his second year of senior and readied himself for the big team's training camp the following autumn.

Bouchard set out from Longueuil, a Montreal suburb on the south shore, for training camp at St. Hyacinthe, 50 miles away. Instead of buying a car, he put his bee money toward materials he and his brother could use to build a house. The decision seemed natural to Bouchard; his parents could live with him in the house rent-free and he could always find some mode of transportation. He made the trip to training camp by bike.

From the first scrimmage, Bouchard, a 6'2", 185-pound defenseman, immediately began leaving impressions. He pounded anyone who ventured on his side, including the team's incumbent policeman Murph Chamberlain, who stubbornly and repeatedly tried to overpower the rookie and get to the net. Each time, Bouchard pasted Chamberlain into the boards a little harder, and when he wasn't battling Chamberlain, Bouchard was hammering any puckhandler who ventured onto his side of the ice. "You must understand," Bouchard says now, a little rueful about manhandling players who would later become his friends, "I wanted to make the team very much."

Bouchard's desire and toughness could not, however, obscure his mediocre skating. It was apparent to everyone that while the rookie made it extraordinarily difficult for any player trying to move the puck around him, he was an awkward, if well-muscled, package of arms and legs. Bouchard's prospects were made even more dubious by general manager Tommy Gorman's preference for a rugged and skilled rookie defenseman named Bert Janke.

It was Bouchard's character as well as his play that eventually landed him a spot with the Canadiens. "The thing was,"

Bouchard recalled, "[Canadiens' coach] Dick Irvin liked me better. This guy, Bert Janke, was walking around with a big cigar in his mouth and Dick Irvin wasn't a smoker and I was not a smoker. Janke was maybe a little cocky and Dick Irvin didn't like that style. I stayed with the Canadiens, Janke went to the farm club in Washington but he lost an eye when he was hit by a stick. I felt sorry for him, I think he would have been up eventually, playing with me."

In his first regular-season game, Bouchard shut down elegant Toronto Maple Leafs' forward Sweeney Schriner. Frustrated by Schriner's inability to beat a rookie defenseman, Leafs' coach Hap Day urged Schriner to try the other side, which he did, blowing by Red Goupille and scoring. Day had made his point, but so had Bouchard.

Frank Selke, who succeeded Gorman in 1946, saw great value in Bouchard. Whenever someone criticized Bouchard's plodding gait, Selke delivered a stock promise. "That boy," he would say, "stays as long as I do."

Within a couple of seasons, Bouchard matured into a fairly smooth defender, but it was his physical strength that set him apart. He gained 20 pounds to peak at 205 pounds and stood as one of the biggest men in the league. Butch had grown into "Big Butch."

"When I first saw his body, I couldn't believe it," remembered former teammate Dickie Moore. "It was like he was chiseled out of stone. He had the biggest shoulders and the smallest waist I had ever seen."

"I don't think Butch was as agile as the big men are today," said Moore, "but no one could go by him on the boards. He would lead them there and when they tried to get between him and the boards, well it was too bad for them." "So strong," said Maple Leafs' Hall-of-Famer Ted Kennedy. "If he happened to get you along the fence, well, you were going to come out second best, but he wouldn't be one of these guys who would run you into the fence to hurt you. He'd rub you out, that's all."

In order to make the most of his skating, Bouchard studied positioning carefully. "In our era, Butch was a very big man and he covered the rink very well," Kennedy said. "I never saw him caught out of position; he played his position very well and by doing so, it didn't necessitate a great deal of skating."

Even with the Canadiens, Bouchard's entrepreneurial streak was never quite quelled. "Butch was a very slow-talking guy, a guy who always talked sense and he had a dry, dry humor," remembered Reardon. "One time, [after] Murph Chamberlain bought his farm and he had something the matter with the roof so Butch organized a working bee and we all went out there, trying to help Murph. Anyway, we get there and Butch has got his good clothes on. He said 'Kenny, you don't expect me to work. Someone has to watch over these guys.' That was Big Butch."

Bouchard kept watch on the ice as well. While he scored 11 goals in the wartime season of 1944–45, it was his stout defense that made him such an invaluable player. He provided the defensive conscience for his more offensively minded partners Kenny Reardon and Tom Johnson, both of whom thrived when paired beside him.

Bouchard's career spanned an era in the NHL where some of the most rugged players—Gordie Howe, Maurice Richard and Ted Lindsay—were also some of the league's preeminent stars. "You didn't have the goons you saw later on," said Reardon. "Each team had a policeman and he was generally the biggest guy on the team and he was definitely the toughest. And he wasn't a brawler. If things got out of hand, he'd step up to the other team and say, 'Hey boys, let's settle this thing down.' Bouchard was not a rough player but he was so big and strong, he could handle himself very well."

Bouchard's status as one of the league's toughest players was established early and never challenged. As a result, he averaged slightly more than a penalty minute per game over his 15 NHL seasons. "I don't think I've ever seen him fight but we had all heard that he could really go," said Kennedy. "Not only was he big, he was courageous as well."

By the late 1940s, Bouchard's wry humor and concern for his teammates had made him hugely popular. Even during Toe Blake's captaincy, it fell to Bouchard to speak and conduct the introductions at the club's banquets.

In 1948–49, his eighth season with the club, Bouchard was named captain. A broken leg had ended Blake's career late in January of the previous season. Goalie Bill Durnan served as captain for the rest of the year but he, quite reasonably, felt that mediating disputes and kicking out shots was too onerous a combination and resigned the job as soon as the season ended.

The Canadiens held a team vote and unanimously elected Bouchard. "That made me happy because, to tell you the truth, I don't agree with management nominating you," Bouchard said. "When it's the players, I can respond to the players, not be a yes-man for the proprietor. I'm not a yes-man."

Bouchard has not changed his view and thinks that initial

mistake in process—letting management choose the captain—led to the problems Mike Keane encountered during his short tenure as captain in 1995–96. "When [Canadiens' then-general manager] Serge Savard nominated Keane, it was a mistake," Bouchard said. "It should go to a vote. The captain should be voted on by the players. He represents the players, why not be voted on by the players?"

Bouchard has limited sympathy for Keane, whose comment that learning to speak French was unnecessary doomed his captaincy and led to his trade to the Colorado Avalanche. "I have nothing against Keane, he's a nice chap, but he made a mistake when he said 'I don't speak French, why should I?' That's stupid, he should have said, 'I don't speak French but I'll try to learn.' That would have been much brighter. If I was nominated in Toronto and I could not speak English, I would say 'I don't speak English, but I'd like to learn.' "

Bouchard wore the C for only 27 games before he tore cartilage in his left knee during a game in November of 1948. He had taken a bride that summer, 20-year-old beauty Marie Claire MacBeth, who distinguished herself marvelously as a hockey wife by agreeing to incorporate a barnstorming tour through western Canada into her honeymoon. Now with a young wife and plans for a family, the career he had built so painstakingly was threatened. Bouchard, who had sold his bee business a few years before, took much of his hockey money and spent his season-long convalescence opening a restaurant on Rue de la Maisonneuve, a stone's throw from the Forum. The restaurant, Chez Butch Bouchard, would become a mecca for the Canadiens and their fans, and the site of countless player stags and wedding receptions.

Surgery and Bouchard's usual single-minded attitude toward conditioning helped him rehabilitate his knee and he was back the following season.

As a captain, Bouchard tended to his teammates as a shepherd tends to his flock. When a player was short of money on the road, he went to Bouchard, who always brought along a little extra for emergencies. It was a practice Jean Beliveau would note and incorporate into his captaincy. Bouchard would not wait to be asked for help; if he saw a young player struggling he would drag him out after practice to correct his mistakes.

When a young Dickie Moore made what he believed to be off-the-record remarks critical of Canadiens' coach Dick Irvin that appeared in a Toronto newspaper, it was Bouchard who defused the situation by taking Moore aside, reminded him of the dangers of being flip around reporters, and then smoothed things over with management.

Bouchard was a leader by example and a player's advocate by inclination. "You had to be an example to the players, you had to be a good worker, but in my case, I went a little harder than that. If a player got in trouble, I'd try to help him."

"He was a good captain because he gave of himself," said onetime teammate Howard Riopelle. " I never heard him criticize anybody but when the time would require it, he would make it known that he wanted some more effort. Overall, it was what he did for the club himself through example, of leading a club through extra effort. I always really admired him for that."

Often, for Bouchard, absorbing Irvin's scathing criticism in front of his peers, was the toughest part of his captaincy. Irvin respected Bouchard, but his coaching style was largely based on confronting the team's most important players whenever a tolerance of losing seemed to be developing. For captains in the six-team NHL, withstanding abuse from coaches was often part of the job description. "In some ways, I always felt he resented Dick Irvin a bit," said Riopelle. "Irvin knew, guys like myself were there to fill in and he wouldn't bother you too, too much. Guys like Doug Harvey and Bouchard, these guys could make the difference and he would really light into them in the dressing room."

"Nowadays, a player would never take that but when you were the captain, you were supposed to lead by example and sometimes that example is by taking all the abuse the coach can give you," Bouchard said. "It's supposed to rebound off the captain and the other players say 'We don't want this guy to go through this again, we've got to get going.'"

Bouchard, a proud man, found holding his tongue excruciatingly difficult and while he still will not criticize Irvin, the memory of those public dressing-downs continues to rankle. But Irvin's instinct was proven correct; Bouchard's ability to absorb punishment was an inspiration inside the dressing room and out.

"The biggest quality in Emile," said Marie Claire, "has always been courage. I don't mean being foolish and reckless, I mean living up to your responsibilities and taking responsibility for what you have to face." For Bouchard, that meant everything from accepting the blizzard of appearances the Canadiens arranged through the season to staring down the opponent's toughest player in a hostile rink. He was a superb captain and through it all, there was always a measure of dry humor. Bouchard once found himself standing beside referee Red Storey as Forum fans, angered over a blown call, pelted the official with peas. "Don't worry, Red," Bouchard said cheerily, "as soon as someone throws some lard, I'll make you up a nice pot of soup."

Bouchard regularly shucked off incidents of obvious prejudice. When opponents taunted him and called him a Frog, Bouchard shot back and called them the first racial epithet that came to mind—even if his guesses were wildly inaccurate.

Referee Georges Gravelle and Bouchard were once speaking French during a stoppage in play. Sid Abel, then the Red Wings' captain, skated over and wanted to know what they were speaking about. "If you want to know," needled Bouchard, "why don't you learn to speak French?" Abel became incensed and relayed the conversation to coach Jack Adams, who complained to the league. A few days later, the NHL ruled conversations between referees and captains had to be conducted in English.

The edict proved too much for Bouchard to resist. "The next time I saw Gravelle, I tried to speak to him in French at center ice. He said 'Get away from me, Mr. Campbell said I wasn't allowed to speak French.' I thought to hell with it, so I chased him all around the rink, speaking French to him."

Bouchard retired in 1956, at the age of 36. The Canadiens won two Stanley Cups in the six seasons Bouchard wore the C and he led the league in fewest goals against for seven of his 15 seasons. Bouchard, a three-time first-team all-star, wound up with 193 points in 781 games. All told, he played on five Cup winners. Bouchard was inducted into the Hall of Fame in 1966.

Even when he retired and had no official affiliation with the club, Bouchard's role as godfather to young players continued unabated. Veterans and rookies alike knew they had a willing ear in Bouchard. To keep players hungry for playoff money, the Canadiens generally paid less salary than the other five NHL teams. When André Pronovost was traded from Montreal to Boston during the 1960–61 season, he was mindful of the dim prospects of earning playoff money with the hapless Bruins and wondered if he should ask his new team for a higher base salary. He took his question to then-captain Doug Harvey, and the two visited Bouchard for his advice. Bouchard listened solemnly, suggested a figure and days later, Pronovost got his raise.

"When players got into difficulties with the organization we would often go to Butch," said Pronovost. "He was close to the organization but he was still able to give us really good advice." Unwilling to break a winning and time-honored formula, Pronovost called Bouchard for advice in 1995 when he was facing heart surgery similar to the kind undergone by Bouchard. "He guided you and I tried to emulate him," said Dickie Moore. "To this day, I still admire him, still admire his leadership."

By the time Bouchard retired as a player, Chez Butch Bouchard employed 85 people and attracted such big-name performers as Charles Aznavour. The use of the restaurant for club functions kept Butch and Marie Claire inside the swirl of life with the Canadiens.

Frugal when spending on himself, Butch was one of the city's softest touches. Many requests for help were legitimate; on several occasions, Bouchard helped bankroll an eye operation for the children of employees. Often stories were made up, but even when fooled, Bouchard refused to complain. "I'd rather be happy with myself and be fooled," Bouchard told Marie Claire when she scolded him for being taken.

Bouchard began to encounter heart problems in 1976 and underwent bypass surgery in 1981. Those heart problems, and the heavy workload that running the restaurant entailed prompted the Bouchards to sell the business in 1982. Bouchard was elected to several terms as an alderman for Longueuil. But his heart problems and a belated desire for a quieter life led him to Florida.

Marie Claire and Butch remain a formidable tandem. In her 48th year of marriage, Marie Claire was asked to describe life with her husband. "Twenty-eight of them," she laughed, "were the best years of my life."

When the Canadiens closed the Forum with a symbolic passing of the torch, Bouchard, the oldest living captain, began the procession from the dressing room in which he had presided so judiciously. And when Maurice Richard was overcome by the ovation he received at the ceremony, it was Bouchard who artfully gave his former teammate a moment's reprieve by sauntering over to him and, with the flair of an old vaudevillian, delivering a handkerchief .

Dickie Moore, standing just a few feet away, laughed with the rest. "Nobody else but Butch could have gotten away with that," said Moore. "But with him, people take it in the context that it was meant. You know, he still comes over to my business and tells me that he's proud of me. And I'll tell you something else, I still love hearing him say it."

CHAPTER 3

MAURICE RICHARD

CAPTAIN 1955–1960

CHAPTER 3

MAURICE RICHARD

CAPTAIN 1955–1960

S ometimes, not often, but sometimes, Maurice Richard finds himself shouting at strangers. "When I go out on the street, people look at me, but they're often too shy to say something so I say 'Good day' or 'Bonjour,'" Richard is saying as he sits in his agent's office in a Laval Industrial Park. "And sometimes, I get mad if they don't say anything. I'll shout at them, 'I just said hello, why don't you answer me?' Most of the time, they're just too shy."

This is the glorious conundrum in being Maurice Richard; you are not subject to casual greetings, only testimonials. The same people too intimidated to greet Rocket Richard spoke through their ovations at an old-timer's game, at the opening of the new Molson Centre, and for almost seven minutes at the closing of the Montreal Forum. No small talk, only homage. Wave after wave of applause, applause when he gestured for the people to stop, applause when the great man wiped a tear from his eye, applause unlike that ever accorded him.

"I didn't know what to say or do," Richard said, the pride and excitement still fresh in his voice two months later. "I tried to stop the crowd from clapping but they kept going just the same. It was the first time I had an ovation like that and I had three in the same week."

Somewhere between 1960, when he retired as a player, and the closing of the Forum in March of 1996, Maurice Richard passed from being the most electrifying hockey player of his era into something far grander. If anything, the applause grows with each passing year and the spiraling level of devotion surprises even the man himself. "I never thought the fans would do that, especially the young fans," Richard said of the ovations. "A lot of young people had never seen me play." Indeed, no one under 35 can remember his reign and no one under 50 was old enough to witness his crowning glory, 50 goals in 50 games.

And yet, the continual heightening of Richard's popularity is by no means new. In 1983, when the Montreal newspaper *La Presse* celebrated its 100th anniversary, readers were asked to name the men of the century. The answers were singer Felix Leclerc and Maurice Richard.

He was the greatest, most charismatic player on the most gloriously successful team in sports history and to understand the legend that is Maurice Richard, you must comprehend the myth of the Montreal Canadiens. The Canadiens are not only a business, they are a trust, a living, breathing value system. Hockey is often described as a religion in Montreal, but the comparison is a poor one. The Canadiens are bigger; their appeal and their hold are far more wide-reaching. In fact, there is a compelling argument to be made that if the sovereignty movement hasn't replaced the Roman Catholic

Church as the fundamental article of faith in the cradle of Canadian Catholicism, the Montreal Canadiens have.

"In the history of Quebec, there have been two great institutions, the Catholic Church and the Montreal Canadiens," noted *La Presse* columnist Réjean Tremblay, the dominant writer in the Francophone sport media. "Religion would like to be like the Canadiens. The Church has lost some prestige, but the Canadiens are an institution."

To many Canadiens fans, the effects of God's hand, hidden in a secular modern world, are apparent when they gaze heavenward at the Forum or now, at the Molson Centre. They see 24 championship banners, almost twice the number of any other NHL team. The Dallas Cowboys may be America's Team but God has always favored the Montreal Canadiens; to the Habs' faithful it is the only explanation for those 24 Stanley Cups. Guy Lafleur answered unequivocally when the question was put to him. "Do people here think God helps the Montreal Canadiens?" said Lafleur. "I think so. I really do."

But the Richard mystique is not only spiritual, it is also sporting, nostalgic and perhaps most importantly, political. His story is the classic tale of the underdog. Richard was not a big man; he entered the league at 5'10½" and 160 pounds, which was about the league norm at the time, and smaller than a later waifish talent named Wayne Gretzky.

Despite his nickname, Richard was not the finest skater of his era. He moved laterally extremely well but there were many, including his brother, Henri, who were markedly faster. He was not a dazzling stickhandler and while his shot was extremely heavy and accurate, it paled in comparison to the rockets Bobby Hull would casually unload a few years later. Yet Maurice Richard became the NHL's all-time top goalscorer and the most charismatic player of his or any other generation. Never the NHL's best talent, he was still the best player where and when it mattered most, from the blue line in, with the puck on his stick, with the game on the line. "He was a hero in that the way he did things was heroic," said Frank Selke, Jr., a publicity director with the Canadiens during Richard's tenure. "Everything he did had a different touch than what anyone else did."

Richard once carried burly Detroit defenseman Earl Seibert on his back for several strides before scoring. When he got to the bench, Seibert was berated by Detroit coach Jack Adams. "Mr. Adams," Seibert said. "I weigh over 200 pounds. Any guy who can carry me on his back from the blue line to the net deserves to score."

"That desperation he played with, it was God's gift," said longtime teammate Dickie Moore. "He was gifted to score goals, gifted to be the king of the castle."

The greatest Montreal Canadien was indomitable and prideful, petty and courageous. He was born into poverty and made his own way to fame. Richard had the perfect disposition for a hockey player, possessing an all-consuming competitiveness and a compulsion to be the best.

Being the greatest came with a price, and not just the largely pleasurable responsibilities of celebrity. "Yes, I guess all I've got today is from hockey," he once told an interviewer, "but you never get as much as you put in." The cost to Maurice Richard is an homage that both attracts him and repels him, elevates and constricts him. He loves the unique fame that brought him the Forum standing ovations. "I like to meet people, the day people don't ask me for autographs when I'm out is the day I'll stay home," Richard said. But he nonetheless chafes over the distance his aura imposes on those he meets on the sidewalk. He is flattered by the attention of interviewers, but burdened with the chore of trying to remember goals he forgot seconds after scoring them.

Maurice Richard insists he is not unhappy with who he is. But he does grow weary of the demands. "I'm not tired," he said. "Sometimes, I'm fed up. I like to be alone. If I can take two or three days off, I'm fine again."

Richard regards his status as a symbol of Quebec pride with ambivalence. When he reached the NHL, Richard knew precisely two English words, "yes" and "no," and his struggles with autocratic Anglo NHL president Clarence Campbell have long since passed into a metaphor for the battles of French-speaking Quebeckers in a province that was largely dominated by the English. "Before René Lévesque, before Lucien Bouchard, before Robert Charlebois, he was the first symbol in a time for people, then known as French Canadians, now known as Québécois," said Réjean Tremblay. "Maurice Richard was the symbol for the little people, the French Canadian who went with his lunchbox to the factory of the English Canadian. The grandfather told his story to the father, who told the story to his children. The tradition has not been lost."

"For French people," said Camil Desroches, a longtime Canadiens publicity director, "he was our flag. We didn't have a flag, we had Maurice Richard." Richard accepts that description, but not the link, obvious to some, between his stubborn insistence on independence and that of half the people who live in his home province.

"I'm comfortable with being a symbol of French pride," is as political a statement as he will make. Richard has never endorsed the politicization of his story and has kept his political thoughts to himself. "I was," Richard has often said, "just a hockey player."

In *The Flying Frenchmen*, an autobiography in English written with New York writer Stan Fischler, Richard said he could very easily have played in an NHL city other than Montreal. "I know many writers have said that the Rocket couldn't think of playing anywhere but in Montreal," wrote Richard. "They believed that I represented the French-speaking people of Quebec and that I couldn't conceive of playing for the English-speaking Maple Leafs. However, if I had to leave Montreal because of a trade I think I would have played in any of the other cities without hesitation and if I had a choice of the five I would have picked Toronto."

Richard's potent appeal has never been exploited by the political figures who have courted him throughout his life. "He could have easily been the prime minister of Quebec or the mayor of Montreal," said Jean Roy, his longtime agent and friend. "But he always said he did not have the knowledge or the education to do the job. His closest friends were all English-speaking persons, from Montreal and from out of Montreal. He was as close to them as to any French Canadian. For him there was no difference, they were all Canadian and he was a Canadian."

The timing of Richard's greatest moments coincided with more than the burgeoning Francophone rage that was the Quiet Revolution. He was a hero not just in a province but in a country desperately looking for one. "We had come out of a

Depression, right into a World War and people's lives were being turned upside down," said Selke. " We wanted a touch-stone, a guy to believe in, a unique person who could make us feel secure."

Radio and newspapers that carried Richard's exploits enjoyed halcyon times in the early stages of his career. Richard was 31 years old and still in his prime in 1952 when television began delivering his image into living rooms across the country.

Analysis is a task for which Richard has little inclination; he has no real explanation for his charisma. When asked why his fame has flowered rather than waned with time, he says it's because he made many appearances after his retirement. It's a stock answer furnished to move an interview on to the next question. He may or may not know the answer: Richard is too busy living through his fame to spend too much time trying to understand it. Like working the corners or shadow-ing the other team's top player, that has always been someone else's job.

On the day of his interview, Richard wore casual slip-on shoes, grey slacks and a Canadiens jacket. His skin looked ruddy and fresh, so did the massive hands. He remains a sub-stantial man, his movements in speaking or walking are not fluid, but forceful and sharp. The famous eyes, the ones Toronto writer Scott Young once said you could look through and see the other side of the rink, aren't black but rather green-hazel, slightly misted by age and still absolutely unmis-takable. In the last few years, there have been rumors, mostly prompted by Richard, that he has Alzheimer's Disease but there is no hint of uncertainty or hesitation in his demeanor, only a resigned determination to answer the questions as quickly as he can. "He's fine," said Roy. "Sure, there are things he forgets about hockey 40 years ago, and there's no question about his memory. He's very bright and very smart."

In July of 1994, Lucille Richard, his wife of 51 years and the mother of their seven children, died after a two-year bout with stomach cancer. They met when Maurice was 16 and Lucille 13 and married five years later. All their adult lives, it was Lucille who made the business decisions, Lucille who scolded him for being too soft on the children when they were young. "He's supposed to be so hard, but at home he's gentle and kind, so good to the kids," she once told an interviewer. "Too good, I tell him." Later, it would be Lucille who would be the most dependable link between the Rocket and his grown children. Perhaps most importantly, it was Lucille who served as a calming counterweight during the daily tempest that was his career. In return, Richard was an extraordinarily devoted husband. He never left the hospital when she was admitted for each birth and he tended to her devotedly during her final illness. When Lucille convalesced at home between treatments, Richard would trust no one but himself or his children with her care.

Richard is not a social man. He has a large circle of friends, but his fame has long since made an ordinary social life impossible. He is not particularly close to his siblings. These factors, plus the dependence, endemic to men of his generation, on a wife who cooked and cleaned, meant that Lucille's death left Richard emotionally and practically abandoned. For several months, he was uninterested in eating or attending to the mountain of business affairs she had left behind. "It's going on two years, but it was really hell," said Roy. "When she passed away, he was happy for her because she had suffered so much. When it was through, he was lost and didn't know what to do."

Hoping to find some solace in an old routine, Richard joined a bunch of NHL old-timers for an extensive tour in the winter of 1995. But the 28-day, 23-city junket left him exhausted and frustrated with the reporters who awaited him at every stop. Discouraged and tired, he had even more trouble than usual recalling the past and wondered aloud in front of reporters if he had Alzheimer's Disease.

However, a new relationship has reinvigorated Richard. A 51-year-old friend of one of his daughters had been helping around the house during and after Lucille's illness. The two, who had been friends for decades, began taking walks together and, eventually, dating. They are now living together, and friends find him far more alert and outgoing than he was during his wife's illness. "My life is good. I'm living with another woman I know, a girlfriend of my daughter," Richard said. "Everything is going well, she helps me a lot around the house. I enjoy life." "People thought he should get a woman near his age but nature and things happened this way," said Roy. "Let's face it, at 75 you haven't got the same number of years from when you're 30."

. Richard grew up in the Bordeaux neighborhood of Montreal, in a home built by his father and grandfather. He was the second eldest of six children born to Onesime and Alice Richard, two members of the First World War exodus to the cities by young Francophones all over Quebec. Onesime and Alice left their native Gaspé and settled in Montreal, where Onesime went to work as a carpenter for Canadian Pacific.

After a short time in the Plateau Mont-Royal area, they moved to the Nouveau Bordeaux district, north of the city and across the Rivière des Prairies from Laval.

"It's true, you really do remember all your life where you came from," Richard said. "We had enough to eat but we had some social assistance because my dad would be laid off for four or five years during the Depression."

His parents had diverse personalities and Maurice was more influenced by his father's taciturn manner than his mother's outgoing one. Onesime Richard was an excellent baseball player and his son initially preferred the sport to hockey, but the long winters spent playing on Rivière des Prairies spurred his development.

In his early teens, Richard fell under the tutelage of Paul Stuart, a Francophone Montrealer who was a godfather to French-speaking hockey players in Montreal. Stuart was in charge of the 40 minor teams that played in the mid-town Park Lafontaine. He brought Richard into the league and became one of his earliest promoters. Even then, the hunger that would shape Richard's game was apparent, he needed to score, craved it, from the age of 11 or 12 on. "I was on the ice most of the time, I wanted to score more goals than anyone else," Richard recalled. "I was there to win, every time."

Stuart knew Richard would never be the biggest player on the ice so he resolved to make him one of the toughest. He enrolled Richard, then 14 or 15, in boxing lessons where he was tutored by Harry Hurst, a well-known Montreal boxer. Richard proved himself to be a quick learner and advanced to the Golden Gloves tournament.

Richard couldn't play enough. Some leagues limited the number of teams for which one prospect could play and to get around the regulations, Richard used the name Maurice Rochon. At one point, he was starring for five teams at the same time.

At 17, Richard began to garner attention from former Canadiens great Aurel Joliat and a local coach and friend of Stuart's, Arthur Therrien. Therrien recommended him to the Verdun Maple Leafs, one of the Habs' best junior teams. After one year in Verdun, he spent two years with the Canadiens' senior team, beginning in 1940–41, and endured the most frustrating seasons of his career. In his first year of senior, Richard broke his left ankle. He returned the following year, but then a broken left wrist sidelined him after 20 games. But he came back to score six goals in four playoff games and seemed a shoo-in to advance to the Canadiens, whose roster was depleted by the war effort in 1942–43. Ironically, Richard himself was exempt from the service because of the ankle injury and was therefore free to become a professional athlete. That summer, on the eve of his first NHL season, 21-year-old Richard married 18-year-old Lucille Norchet.

Then, disaster. Richard broke his right ankle in his sixteenth NHL game when Johnny Crawford of the Boston Bruins decked him near the end of his shift. The two fell together and Richard's ankle bent under his body.

Devastated, Richard considered quitting. "I'm either on my ass or in the hospital," he fumed. Compounding his misery was a string of remarks made by Canadiens' coach Dick Irvin and general manager Tommy Gorman, who fed quotes to newspaper reporters questioning whether the young rookie was too fragile to play in the NHL. It was a devastating blow to Richard, whose injuries had been the result of bad luck, not congenital weakness. While the comments were never made to his face, he neither forgot nor forgave them.

"I didn't like hearing that too much," Richard recalled. "That was the trouble with Dick Irvin, if he had something to say he would say it in front of everybody. I never liked Dick Irvin just on account of that."

The next season, 1943–44, Richard began to prove Irvin and Gorman wrong. He missed only 12 games to injury over the next six years. In a move that would make hockey history, Richard bumped a player named Charlie Sands out of the right-wing spot on a line already centered by Elmer Lach; on the left side was 31-year-old Toe Blake.

Richard scored 32 goals that year, his first full season in the league, including five in one game against Toronto, and became the heart of a unit newspaper reporters dubbed the Punch Line.

The troika was one of the best ever assembled. The Punch Line produced over 700 points in four and a half years together before Blake's injured leg and retirement broke them up in 1947. The success of the unit lay in the creativity of its members. "We had plays of our own that nobody knew about, that we worked on when everybody else was gone," said Lach. " 'Maurice,' I said, 'if the puck is in the corner, you get into this area because I'll put the puck in there blind.' It would work." Richard had more than an unparalleled need to score in his favor. A left-hand shot, he had always felt more comfortable on the right side (most right-wingers shot right).

"Maurice, how would I say it, could put the puck through an eye of a needle. Coming off the right wing with the left hand shot gave him a great advantage," said Lach. In that heady second season, Maurice became Rocket, a nickname bestowed upon him by a triumvirate of teammates, Phil Watson, Murph Chamberlain and Ray Getliffe. The name was picked up by reporters and Maurice Richard was the Rocket forever more.

The Canadiens finished first overall in 1943–44 and won the Stanley Cup as Richard scored 12 post-season goals, including five in a four-game sweep of Chicago. That breakthrough season would serve only as a prelude. In his third year, Richard breezed past Joe Malone's record of 44 goals, set with the Canadiens in 1918, the inaugural year of the NHL. Almost as an afterthought, Richard beat Boston's Harvey Bennett on March 18, 1945, to become the first player ever to score 50 goals. He turned the trick in 50 games.

While 50 goals endures as the gold standard for NHL players. Fifty goals in 50 games remains the platinum measure, the final accounting of the game's most prolific scorers. Only Richard, the New York Islanders' Mike Bossy, St. Louis sharpshooter Brett Hull, Wayne Gretzky and Mario Lemieux have managed the feat.

In 1945–46, Richard posted a 27-goal regular season and added his first of a record six post-season overtime goals as the Canadiens handled Boston in five games to claim the Cup. By this time, Richard's compulsion to score overran every area of his life. "He roams around the house, muttering to himself," Lucille once told a biographer. "He gets mad and stays that way until he gets a goal. And even a goal, or a cluster of them, won't make him happy unless the Canadiens win. When he's in a surly mood, all he does is eat."

Richard hated to leave the house when he was in a slump; every second person in the grocery store would remind him of his on-ice troubles. When he was not playing well, his anger settled into a brooding silence that precluded even cursory conversation and even on the road, the pressure was unrelenting. "He had it pretty tough," remembered former Canadien Tom Johnson. "He was about the most vulnerable athlete there was at the time. He couldn't come out to the local bars in Detroit or Toronto with us because there would always be somebody picking a fight with him. He had to pretty well hide if he wanted a quiet beer."

Each rink brought a new barrage of verbal abuse, often coarse and racist. Small wonder then, that Richard often played in a rage. Once, during a game in the 1946–47 season, he decked a New York Ranger with one punch. Not willing to skate away after winning the fight, he raised his stick over the prone Ranger and drove it, again and again, into the ice beside the fallen player.

Richard's fervor sometimes cost his team dearly. In Game Two of the 1947 Stanley Cup finals against Toronto, Richard was sent off for an interference penalty in the first period. The underdog Leafs scored on that power play and Richard was sent off again in the second for his part in a vicious stick-swinging duel with Vic Lynn in which the Toronto forward was badly cut. The Leafs scored two more goals and as soon as Richard left the box, he became embroiled in another stick-swinging incident, this one with Bill Ezinicki. Ezinicki, too, was badly cut and Richard incurred a match penalty and a suspension for the following game. The Canadiens lost 4–0, all on goals incurred with Richard in the penalty box. They never regained their equilibrium and fell in six games. In that series, the league was put on permanent notice that with Richard, an explosion that could sink him and his teammates might come at any time. Even then, some saw the incidents against the Leafs as the beginning of a continuum. "If they had thrown the book at him when he cut Lynn and Ezinicki in 1947," former Toronto and Boston center Fleming Mackell once said, "it might have stopped him and he might have become a greater player because of it."

Like most stars, Richard was shadowed from the moment he stepped on to the ice. "I think if I let Rocket go to the bathroom between games, [Leafs' checking forward Bob] Davidson would be in there with him," complained Irvin. Surprisingly, Richard did not mind the pests—he greatly admired Davidson, for example—and even used them for motivation. "Every time I had someone following me, it made me skate harder, work harder," Richard said.

Referees were more problematic. Canadiens' coach Dick Irvin was a notorious referee baiter and Richard, encouraged to feel victimized by officials, would routinely take matters into his own hands. "I was never the first guy to hit somebody after a bad check but when it did happen, it got in my mind to go after him right away," he said. "A clean hit I didn't mind, a dirty hit, I did mind and 90 percent of the time when I went after a guy, I would be the one who got a penalty."

Toronto captain Ted Kennedy remembered it differently. Every hit, clean, dirty and in-between, he said, tested Richard's patience. "He was the type of guy, even if it was a good, clean bodycheck, he would react. A lot of guys will say, 'OK, I'll get my shot,' but he would react right away. I don't know whether it was Gallic pride or what but particularly in Montreal, if something happened, even though they were clean checks, he would react immediately."

Naturally, that tendency made Richard the subject of even more on-ice attention and the spiral continued unabated. "But, I have to give him credit," Kennedy said. "I never saw him go out to do something mean or dirty to the other team when they had the puck. Never. He never started it, but once it happened, he never backed away. He was a very, very courageous guy."

If a shadow stretching the rules could not harness Richard, perhaps a thug could. The New York Rangers, desperate to stop Richard during his 50-goal year, called up a minor league tough guy named Bob "Killer" Dill to fight Richard. The move backfired: within a few shifts, Richard had knocked Dill unconscious.

Once, in Detroit, Richard slapped a teen-ager across the face who leaned over the glass to taunt him in the penalty box. Richard was without contrition. "The kid was a nasty brat with a filthy tongue," he told reporters. "He stuck his face right up at me yelling at me. I'd slap my own son a lot harder if he dared speak to his elders that way, even at a hockey game." After the game, the Canadiens surrounded Richard to escort him out of the Olympia but the sight of him, the fierce gaze clear even in street clothes as he smacked an empty soft drink bottle against his open palm, erased any possibility of retribution.

Through it all, Richard was a relentless critic of his own performance. An excellent night only heightened fear of a backslide two nights later, and Richard was often furious with himself if he only scored one goal—even in games the Canadiens won. "I had in my mind that I had a lot of chances, some days I would get 12 or 13 shots and only one goal," Richard remembered. "That's when I would think I had a bad night." Not all of Richard's passion was self-induced. On rare occasions when his fervor ebbed, Irvin or a designated teammate would stoke it.

"My dad always believed that some players played better if you made them mad," said Dick Irvin, Jr., the longtime "Hockey Night in Canada" color and play-by-play man. "He always felt guys like the Rocket and Elmer Lach played better if they were upset with the other team. Dad used to say he knew when the Rocket was ready to play—his hair was standing on end."

Irvin would berate Richard and sometimes block the gate when Richard was sent off to cool down by officials. One night, Richard clashed with a rookie referee named Hugh McLean when the young official sent Richard off for slashing after Richard himself had been slashed. Richard chased McLean, demanding an explanation for the one-sided call. Instead McLean tagged Richard with a 10-minute minor for unsportsmanlike conduct. Richard was still furious the next day when, in the lobby of a New York hotel, Canadiens' goalie Gerry McNeil baited him by pointing to McLean, and saying the referee had been loudly mocking him. Richard stormed across the hotel lobby and grabbed McLean by the throat. Miraculously, he avoided a suspension.

Bert Olmstead, who arrived in Montreal 1951, soon became expert at pricking Richard, like a jockey whipping a horse through the final turn. If another line was going well, Olmstead would point it out on the bench. If Richard had been made to look foolish, Olmstead would reinforce the embarassment. "I always knew how to get to Rock. I'd look at Dick Irvin, just before we'd go on the ice," Olmstead said. "If he nodded, I'd get on him. If he didn't, I'd leave him alone. I could handle him, I could get him so mad but it all depended on the moment, how we were going, who was scoring." But the needle was applied on the bench, quietly. "If I had done it in front of anyone else, he would have laid me out," Olmstead said.

The pressure on Richard grew with each season. Competition, even inside the team, was endless. Fights were commonplace at practice, and rivalries between lines was fierce. "If somebody else's line got two goals, we'd have to get three," Olmstead said. Richard did his part, breaking the 40-goal mark three times. In the 1951 playoffs, Richard scored the winning goal in the fourth overtime period in the semi-final opener against Detroit. In Game Two, he added another overtime goal, this one in the third overtime. Despite another overtime winner from Richard in the final against Toronto, the Canadiens fell to the Maple Leafs in five games on a series ended by Bill Barilko's famous overtime goal. In November 1952, Richard scored goal number 325 to pass former Maroon, Boston Bruin and New York American Nels Stewart and he remained the NHL's all-time goalscoring king throughout his career.

The seventh game of the 1952 semi-final against Boston furnished the greatest demonstration of the instinct with which Richard played. For many, it was Richard's finest and most telling moment. Richard was knocked unconscious in the second period when he was hit by powerful Bruins forward Leo Labine and fell headfirst into the knee of Bruins' defenseman Bill Quackenbush. "From the press box," *Montreal Standard* beat man Andy O'Brien wrote later, "we thought his neck was broken." Richard was motionless as he was carried off the ice and didn't move an eyelid as doctors inserted six stitches into his forehead. He didn't get off the training table until he rose and skated to the Canadiens bench late in the third period.

Richard sat beside Elmer Lach on the bench, but since he could not focus on the clock, it fell to his linemate to tell him the score was 1–1 with four minutes left. Moments later, Richard picked up a pass from Butch Bouchard in his own end and ducked past a forechecker at center. He veered to his right and tried to beat Quackenbush wide. Quackenbush, an excellent defenseman, hung with him so Richard shoved him aside with his left arm and drove toward the net. Bob Armstrong, the other Boston defenseman, charged Richard but it was too late. Richard was in on Boston goalie Sugar Jim Henry, himself playing with two black eyes and a broken nose. Richard deked Henry and scored as the Forum crowd went berserk. After the game, Jim Henry and Richard shook hands in a moment that would be preserved in one of hockey's most memorable pictures.

A few minutes into the dressing room celebration, Richard broke into a wild, sobbing convulsion and he was rushed to a training table and sedated. It would be another two hours before the shock had passed and Richard could leave the building. "That beautiful bastard," said *Montreal Herald* writer Elmer Ferguson, "scored semi-conscious."

That goal was the signature scoring play of Richard's career. It came during the vital moments of a playoff game and its drama was breathtaking. Just as typical was how the goal was scored, on a breakneck rush to the net.

Game films of Maurice Richard show a player with tremendous first step acceleration and a backhand better than that of any NHL player today. Richard instructed teammates to lead him a little more than most players with their passes; the extra lean often allowed him to blow by slower, bigger players charged with shadowing him. Only two modern players, Glenn Anderson and Pittsburgh's Jaromir Jagr, drive to the net with anywhere near the authority of Richard and those two have enjoyed the benefits of modern technology, which allows the net to break free if struck with any measure of force. Before detachable nets, driving the net was the single most productive and bonebreaking means of scoring. Aside from his final year or two, Richard never tired of paying the price to score. For 15 of his 18 seasons, Richard finished among the league's top five goalscorers. "It was an unwritten law, that if somebody was sliding early in the net, you'd try to block them," said Canadiens' backup goalie Charlie Hodge, "but still, this guy would go to the net so often, it was unbelievable. It didn't matter how he scored. He used to be the same way in practice, he wouldn't shoot the puck in the net in practice, he'd try to put it through the net."

"People have said he was the best player of all time," said former Red Wing Ted Lindsay, Richard's most virulent on-ice opponent, "and I say no. But, the Rocket from the blue line in was the greatest hockey player of all time. Nobody will ever equal him."

In the millisecond that determines the outcome of a scoring chance, Richard's greatest gift was his impulsiveness; he never knew what he would do before the moment arrived. "If you don't know what you're going to do," he once said, "how can the defenseman?" Canadiens' general manager Frank Selke once spoke eloquently of the difference between Jean Beliveau and Maurice Richard. "With Maurice, his moves are powered by instinctive reflexes. Maurice can't learn from lectures. He does everything through instinct and sheer power. The difference between the two best players in the game today is simply this: Beliveau is a perfectionist, Maurice is an opportunist."

About half of Richard's goals were scored on the backhand. It lacked the velocity of his forehand but was nonetheless tremendously accurate. As he did in his legendary goal against the Bruins, Richard warded off players with his left arm extraordinarily well.

"Since I was a left-handed shot, I carried most of the weight of my stick in my right or upper hand," Richard once told a biographer. "When you carry your stick that way, you have your left arm on the side of the defense. You always have a chance to hold the man off and keep him from reaching at the puck. If I had been playing left wing, it would have been a lot more difficult."

Richard liked to shoot low. "Some players develop a habit of lifting every shot waist-high or higher; that gives the goaler use of his hands which are quicker than his legs, burdened down by those heavy pads plus skates," he wrote in his autobiography. "I'd urge kids to try keeping their shots no more than two feet off the ice." Richard favored a wrist shot over a slap shot and he was gifted with a heavy, accurate shot that he worked on relentlessly. Canadiens' goalie Bill Durnan hated facing Richard's shot in practice. Richard had such strong wrists, he could often keep his hands high on the stick and whip it into the net in much the same way Eric Lindros does today.

Ranger great Rod Gilbert remembered asking Richard about the secret to scoring after a Canadiens practice. Richard spaced a few pucks around the offensive zone and in one motion charged the pucks, pivoted and violently rifled them, one by one, into the net. When he was done, Richard skated up to an awestruck Gilbert. "Kid," he said, "in this league you've got to be able to hit the net."

Richard rarely attempted to stickhandle past a player in neutral ice. He found dishing the puck off and looking for a return pass far preferable, especially with Lach—who assisted on 159 of his goals—on hand and anxious to return the pass. "He really wasn't a great puck carrier," remembered Ted Kennedy. "If he got the puck, he'd move it to the center or the other wing and get into position. If the puck came to him inside the opposition's goal line, forget about the pass. One way or another, forehand or backhand, he was going to get a shot on goal. He would fight to get into position without the puck and then when he got it, he was very difficult to stop. Those eyes would be so focused when he got the puck, they would just shoot the sparks out."

Away from the net, Richard liked to double-back fairly deep into his own territory. He rarely, if ever, handled the puck in his own end and he initiated bodychecks very infrequently. "I have found it usually shakes me up as much as the fellow I have checked," he wrote. Still, while a middling defensive player, Richard was far more diligent than the procession of superstars—Hull, Gretzky, Lemieux—who have followed him and Irvin used him in defensive situations. On a turnover, he always headed back first to his own zone and once there he picked up his man. The Canadiens kept track in 1950–51; while Richard scored 43 goals, his check scored 11 times. Still, Richard rationed his strength for offense. He was, Jean

Beliveau wrote, "a highly-tuned, specialized hockey instrument, not a well-balanced, all-around player."

The Canadiens finally returned to the winner's circle in 1953 but during the first half of Richard's career the NHL was dominated by the Maple Leafs and the Detroit Red Wings. As a 10-year-veteran, Richard had won only two Cups before the Canadiens broke through for another win in 1953 with a five-game triumph over Boston.

Maurice Richard was 33 years old when he entered what would be the defining season of his life, 1954–55, the season of the Richard Riot. Even as he neared his mid-thirties, his temper remained barely in check. The season before, aside from the usual scrapes, he punched out a fan at an exhibition game in Valleyfield. Richard and the Canadiens had been in a foul mood since the previous spring, when they suffered one of their most agonizing losses in dropping the seventh game of the Stanley Cup final to their arch-rival Red Wings in overtime.

The chain of events that led to the Richard Riot began to unfold late in the year when Ted Lindsay was suspended by NHL president Clarence Campbell for four games because he punched a fan during a game. A former NHL referee, Rhodes Scholar and member of the prosecuting team at Nuremberg, Campbell had been gradually attempting to project a big-league image for the NHL, which was engaged in a love-hate relationship with violence that continues to this day. While the suspension seems light now, the move sparked howls of outrage from Detroit. The Red Wings argued Richard had avoided similar sanctions for far more serious actions like the bloody duels with Ezinicki and Lynn. That very season,

Richard had escaped a suspension after hitting a linesman with a glove during a fight. Richard had already paid more fines, $2,000, than any player in NHL history but Campbell felt intense pressure from the front offices of the Detroit Red Wings, Chicago Black Hawks and New York Rangers, all of whom were controlled by the Norris family, to show Richard no leniency the next time Richard exploded.

The Canadiens and Red Wings battled for first place through the season and with little more than a week left, the two teams were tied atop the standings. Going into a game March 13 in Boston, Richard also held a narrow lead over teammate Bernie Geoffrion in the battle for the Art Ross Trophy, awarded to the league's top point-getter.

Given his style, demeanor and the way his coach and some teammates agitated him, another Richard explosion was inevitable. What was surprising was who set it off. Richard and Bruins' defenseman Hal Laycoe had been teammates for just over three seasons in Montreal, and they occasionally saw each other over the summers. Still, the Rocket was in a foul mood going into the game. An aching back had made even minor movement aggravating and late in the contest, he and Laycoe began slamming sticks over each other's heads. It was a wild melee; three times Richard found himself without his stick and used someone else's to get at Laycoe. During the course of the fight, linesman Cliff Thompson grabbed Richard several times and finally separated him from Laycoe before Canadiens' defenseman Doug Harvey bumped the pair and knocked Richard free. Thompson was a former Bruin; he had played 13 games with the club both before and after the Second World War and that was enough to taint him in the eyes of the Richard. When Thompson once again grabbed him, Richard assumed he was trying not so much to restrain as to immobilize him so Laycoe could inflict more damage with his stick. "I didn't have my stick and he was swinging at me," recalled Richard. "The official was holding me from behind and I warned him two or three times. The fourth time," he said, a slight smile creasing his lips, "I turned around and poked him." The two blows left Thompson with a bruise on the cheek and a black eye. Referee Frank Udvari immediately ejected Richard from the game.

It was an extraordinarily serious breach and Richard and the rest of the hockey world expected a similar suspension to the one meted out to Lindsay. But no one expected a penalty that would knock Richard out for the remaining three games of the regular season as well as the balance of the upcoming playoffs.

Three days after the fight, Campbell convened a hearing in the league's Montreal office. The meeting was attended by Richard, Canadiens' assistant general manager Ken Reardon, Laycoe, Boston GM Lynn Patrick and the game officials, including Udvari, and it was conducted entirely in English.

The Norris family, whose Red Wings stood to be the primary beneficiary of a Richard suspension, constituted a majority block of the league. Campbell answered only to the owners and between the incident and the hearing, they had made it clear they expected a lengthy suspension. Richard had supplied his rivals with the very outburst that could be used against him. Frank Selke, Jr., who lived at home and was privy to many of the conversations between his father, Campbell and the other owners, said it was a done deal from the start.

"There's no question the Rocket became a scapegoat," Selke, Jr., said. "The ringleader was [Detroit general manager] Jack Adams, who had a relationship with the Norris family. Nobody would deny that a suspension was legitimate, but not for the playoffs." "I was the best scorer on the Canadiens and we were winning all the time," Richard said simply. "Everyone was working hard to beat us and the other owners didn't want me around for the playoffs."

Campbell provided the perfect villain for Richard and his supporters. With his lawyerly manner and perfectly tailored suits, Campbell moved with the imperious air of the Anglo elite. Throughout his career, Richard suspected Campbell disliked French-speaking people and Campbell's remarks in suspending Richard were laced with condescension. "Whether this type of conduct is the product of temperamental instability or willful defiance of the authority of the game does not matter," Campbell said in announcing his decision. "Richard will be suspended from all games, both league and playoffs, for the balance of the entire season."

History has some constants: the faults attributed to those without power by those in charge never change: the powerless are invariably viewed as stupid, even sub-human, carnal and brutish. There was no mistaking the intent of the words "temperamental instability." Campbell was saying that while Richard may have been driven by his racial identity toward violence, that would not absolve him from prosecution.

The reaction to the suspension was swift, visceral and racially divisive. "L'Affaire Richard," with all its obvious symbolism—autocratic Anglo manager against French-speaking working-class hero—became a cultural milestone in the evolution of Quebec. "You had in Quebec at the time what political scientists call a cultural division of labor," said Hudson Meadwell, chair of the political science faculty at McGill University. "The bosses were English and typically, they managed French working-class people. Maurice Richard, a French-speaking hockey player from Bordeaux embodied something no one else embodied: he was a populist figure. When he was brought down to earth the way he was, people thought it was directed at them. An attack on Maurice Richard was an attack on Francophones."

The violent reaction to the Richard incident was a dramatic manifestation of growing pride and restlessness among French Quebeckers about the division of power, an anger that would fuel the Quiet Revolution in the late 1950s and early 1960s. English-speaking Montrealers, many for the first time, saw their city divided along racial lines and felt first-hand a measure of the pent-up rage of French-speaking Quebeckers.

Andy O'Brien later wrote that it was the first time he had felt real conflict between French and English in Montreal. "The French—almost to a man (as well as woman and child)—rallied behind the Rocket. They were bitter—deep down bitter—about a penalty that they thought excessively harsh."

That Saturday, the Red Wings visited the Forum. Campbell attended the game with his fiancée, Phyllis King, but did not take his usual seat in the arena's south side, near the goal judge, until late in the first period. By then, the demoralized Canadiens were losing 4–1. Soon Campbell was pelted with debris from the stands. One man smashed tomatoes in his chest, another made a motion to shake his hand and then punched him. Seconds later, at 9:11 p.m., a tear-gas canister exploded near Campbell. The person who fired the tear-gas was never found but the canister was the brand sold to the Montreal police by the product's manufacturer.

Richard had attended the game and when the trouble started, he left his seat to meet Lucille in a prearranged spot, the Forum infirmary. There, he saw Campbell speaking with the chief of police, Tom Leggatt. "I looked at him but the inspector said 'Rocket, don't even talk to him.' I didn't do anything and I wouldn't have," Richard smiled at the retelling. "I just wanted to talk to him."

On Campbell's order, the game was quickly declared a forfeit and thousands of fans spilled into Rue Ste Catherine, right into a pro-Richard demonstration. The combination of the protest, the tear-gas and the panic it struck ignited the crowd and triggered a four-hour rampage—the infamous Richard Riot. Between 5,000 and 10,000 people participated in the riot. Hundreds of stores were looted and vandalized along a 15-block area and 12 policemen and 25 civilians were hurt. Damage exceeded $100,000. Though badly outnumbered, police who reached the scene managed to arrest 37 men. All but eight pleaded guilty to minor charges such as disturbing the peace and disrupting traffic. The next day, Richard, speaking from the Canadiens' dressing room via radio, issued an appeal for calm. His words, along with a dramatically increased police contingent, ended any possibility of further violence.

With the forfeit, the Red Wings claimed a two-point lead in the standings and eventually won the regular-season crown by five points. The Habs' first shot at a regular season title in eight years had been swept away by the crowd and the passion of the man who inspired it.

Bernie "Boom Boom" Geoffrion, warned by teammates Doug Harvey and Jean Beliveau not to let up with the regular season title still in doubt, climbed past Richard and won the scoring title 75 points to 74. It was the second time Richard had lost a share of the scoring crown by a point. Prior to the team's first playoff game against Boston, an out-of-uniform Richard was accorded a lengthy standing ovation. Geoffrion, however, was booed heavily when presented with the Hart Trophy. The venom directed toward Geoffrion for usurping Richard was so intense that he feared for his family's safety and took on police protection.

Richard's position on his suspension has never wavered. "I should have been suspended for 10 or 15 games the next season, but not for the playoffs," he said. Without Richard, the Canadiens lost the final to Detroit in seven games. As for the scoring title, in his book, Richard wrote: "I certainly can't blame the Boomer. He was trying to win games for the team. He was also playing to win the scoring championship, but there were a few assists that he received over the season that were cheap. When I think of them and the chance that it was my last chance at the title, I can't help but feel resentful." It was one of the most telling quotes Richard has ever provided. The words reflected the man himself: laudably honest and dishearteningly petty, he possessed equal measures of greatness and frailty.

In the aftermath of the riot, Campbell disputed assertions, including those from Richard, that by attending the game he provoked the outburst. He was particularly incensed that

Montreal mayor Jean Drapeau laid the blame at his door and criticized the mayor in a typically lawyerly rebuttal. "Does the Mayor suggest I should have yielded to the intimidation of a few hoodlums?" Campbell asked. "What a strange and sorry commentary from the chief magistrate of our city who was sworn to uphold the law and who as senior officer of the civic administration is responsible for the protection of the persons and property of the citizens through our police force."

The Richard Riot changed everything. Campbell, who remained in office until 1977, considered the Richard suspension the watershed in his office's growth. "It's funny, but until I made the decision to suspend Rocket Richard from the playoffs of 1955, I was never acknowledged as the head of the NHL," Campbell said in 1970. "I could have fined the Rocket $250 but he was such a hero, he would have received $2,500 donations from fans. In the Montreal Forum I was pelted with bottles and garbage, but that's when my office first took on some meaning."

Campbell died in June of 1984 at the age of 78. Richard went to the funeral. When asked for a comment on the events of 1955, he said Campbell was wrong. "It was President Campbell," he said, "who incited that crowd."

While Campbell's presidency would flourish, Dick Irvin, Sr.'s tenure with the Canadiens had ended. Selke, although a great friend of Irvin's, had long chafed over Irvin's tactic of aggravating Richard. "You can no longer coach the team," Frank Selke, Sr., told Irvin. "Your handling of the Rocket cost us the Stanley Cup. There is a place for you inside the organization as long as you want to stay but you are not to coach." Instead, Irvin bolted to Chicago.

That season also marked the end of Butch Bouchard's stewardship and it fell to Richard to assume the captaincy of the Canadiens. There was, however, a caveat: leave the fighting to someone else. Selke pointed out that at 34, Richard no longer needed to fight and should instead conserve energy that could be better used scoring.

More importantly, Selke installed Toe Blake as his coach. Blake had played with Richard and the two had a mutual respect. And Blake, like Selke, believed that Irvin's handling of Richard had been patently incorrect. "If I ever say anything that hurts you, don't say anything to the press," Blake told Richard. "Wait, and come and see me and we'll talk about it."

Blake knew his old linemate was fueled by a constant and enormous desire to compete and that aggravating him only loosened Richard's grip on his emotions, and often, the game. Instead, Blake worked to calm Richard down; his line changes often revolved around defusing potential explosions and from behind the bench, he reminded him to stay calm. "I often had to cool him out, right on the bench," Blake once told a reporter. "He glared at me, but he took it. Maybe because I was an old linemate and he knew we had been through a lot together, and, most likely, because he didn't want to make my first season as an NHL coach tougher."

A measure of volatility was siphoned away from Richard's game but, as Blake had suspected, his productivity did not dip. While his penalty minutes dropped from a career high of 125 to 89, Richard scored 38 goals, the same total he collected in the year of the riot.

Richard's captaincy coincided with some of the club's greatest campaigns. Richard won the Stanley Cup in each of his remaining five years and the Canadiens of the late 1950s assumed their place as the predominant dynasty in NHL history.

Richard aged beautifully in his role. The captaincy massaged his pride and accorded him a formal respect that acknowledged not only his ability but his standing within the team and the organization. The captaincy, Richard said, "was never really that important to me. Representing the players was important, but apart from that I saw my job really as doing my best. I didn't speak very good English so what I did on the ice had to motivate the players." "The Rocket led by example, by putting the puck in the net," said Dickie Moore. "All the players in the room were in awe of him, they were in awe of how forceful he was in pleasing the people." Players like Beliveau and Doug Harvey handled the social elements of the job with which Richard did not feel comfortable. And while he now wore the C, the presence of Beliveau, Geoffrion, Doug Harvey and Jacques Plante meant that Richard, still formidable and the focal point of the Canadiens, was no longer the primary target of every opposition game plan. That left him to do what he did best. In the 1957 final against Boston, Richard scored four times in Game One, including three goals in the second period as the Canadiens won in five.

In 1958, the Canadiens handled Boston in six games, and the playoffs remained Richard's stage. Richard scored 11 goals in the post-season and collected his sixth overtime goal in the playoffs.

Age, however, was beginning to bring the Rocket down by 1959. His weight ballooned to about 200 pounds and he would not allow himself to be weighed at the Canadiens' training camp. Blake, who inherited Irvin's fanaticism for conditioning, nevertheless shrugged his shoulders and left his old linemate alone. As well, injuries were beginning to pile up. Richard hurt his right elbow at training camp in 1956 and had minor surgery to remove bone chips that forced him out of the lineup for seven games. A severe Achilles' tendon injury, incurred when Maple Leafs' defenseman Marc Reaume fell over Richard and cut his foot with his skateblade, forced him out of 42 more games the following year.

A broken leg prevented him from playing much of the 1958–59 season and he played only briefly in the Stanley Cup final as the Canadiens polished off Toronto in five games. For the first time, Richard was held off the scoresheet in a playoff round. More injuries, this time a severe fracture on the left side of his face, knocked him out for 19 games in 1959–60. While he scored 19 goals, and another in the Cup final to push his playoff goals total to 34, the Richard era was clearly ending.

"If you needed the money badly or we were desperate for manpower, we probably would be urging you to play another season," Frank Selke told Richard in the summer of 1960. "Since neither of these conditions exist, I must tell you we are concerned about the possibility of you getting hurt badly."

At 39, Maurice Richard attended one more training camp in September. Early in camp, he scored four blazing goals against Jacques Plante in practice. "It was his way," wrote O'Brien, "of saying goodbye" and for the first time in 18 years, the Montreal Canadiens faced life without Maurice Richard.

Richard retired with a record 544 goals, 83 of which, or 15 percent, were game winners. This career goal-scoring record stood only three years, however, before Gordie Howe bettered it. Today, Maurice Richard's name is missing from the record books in the individual game, season, and career regular-season records. But he remains the all-time playoff overtime goal leader with six, one more than Glenn Anderson. Richard's achievement of five goals in a playoff game has never been bettered, although five players, including Mario Lemieux, have equalled the trick. He also shares a record four points in one period with nine other players. In October of 1960, the Canadiens retired Richard's jersey, number 9, and the following summer the Hockey Hall of Fame waived its three-year waiting period to install Richard as a member.

Richard's relations with the Canadiens were typically volatile. After his retirement as an active player, he assumed a front-office job with the club but most former players were considered figureheads. Beliveau, not Richard, was clearly the organization's choice as its future spokesman. The banquet circuit that Beliveau would later master with such grace was an uncomfortable fit for Richard. In Boston one night, he brought a B'nai B'rith dinner to an awkward pause with this speech: "I'm happy to be back in Boston. I came here regularly in my eighteen years as a player. We beat the Bruins eight or nine times in the playoffs. We always won. Guess that's why I like it here so much." And with that, he sat down.

When Sam Pollock took over management of the Canadiens in 1964, Richard was promoted to vice president but saw his input even less valued than before. "Apparently, the new administration didn't want me to do anything. I was just a showpiece sitting around the Forum like a potted plant!" Richard would later write. "They didn't even show me the courtesy of asking my advice about some of the players whom I knew so much about. The only thing I was to do was go to the occasional banquet and make a few speeches, at half the salary I made before." Five years into his stint with the Canadiens, Richard quit. Tired of not being consulted he left the office one afternoon to cut his grass. When he was chastised the next day, he resigned.

Richard had made about $350,000 from playing and endorsements, so he had money for his own enterprises. He began a fishing line business and lent his name to a restaurant.

A decade after the end of his playing career, Richard approached even an exhibition game with the same trademark intensity. "The fire was still there. He never considered any game a lark to go out and put on an exhibition of fun," remembered Ted Kennedy. "He was out there to score goals. His ability wasn't there as much as it was, he was older and wasn't skating as well, but the intensity was always there."

To keep himself in shape, Richard refereed in leagues around Montreal and he did make one official foray back into pro hockey. The World Hockey Association's fledgling Quebec Nordiques signed him to be their coach upon their formation in 1972. Richard signed his contract at the Quebec City Hall and even walked in a small parade but the pairing did not last. The trip to Quebec took almost three hours by car and Lucille wanted to stay in Montreal. Richard was ill suited to coach: he was 51 and he had little inclination for the minutiae of strategy and motivational tactics that are a coach's stock-in-trade. His bench career lasted two games, a win and a loss, and the stress on him was obvious.

"We can't ask Maurice Richard to die behind the bench," said Marius Fortier, the club's general manager, when Richard left. "And it's obvious that this has become a superhuman task, beyond his powers. He has visibly lost weight since he's been with us. His morale is very low."

The Canadiens canceled his complimentary pass when Richard took the Quebec job and because of his strained relations with the club, he was absent from ceremonial nights held for Jean Beliveau and Toe Blake, as well as Frank Mahovlich. But when Richard agreed to attend his brother Henri's night in 1973 his pass was returned and Richard and the Canadiens reconciled. In 1980, he was put on the payroll as a goodwill ambassador and he has enjoyed good relations with the Canadiens ever since.

Age carries its inevitable humiliations and in 1993, Richard dropped the Stanley Cup in a ceremony at the Forum. But the Rocket, wrote *Toronto Star* columnist Milt Dunnell, surely had to be forgiven for dropping the Cup once. After all, he had drunk from it eight times before. "He came into the alumni room and said, 'Did you see me make an ass of myself?'" remembered Bert Olmstead. "I said 'Rock, there is nothing you could do to make an ass of yourself . . .'" His old linemate paused to consider the mystery that is Rocket Richard. "I don't know whether he understood me or not."

CHAPTER 4

DOUG HARVEY

CAPTAIN 1960–1961

CHAPTER 4

DOUG HARVEY

CAPTAIN 1960–1961

D oug Harvey died in December of 1989 in a Montreal
hospital from cirrhosis of the liver and if he is remembered at all by younger fans, it's because of an erroneous
footnote in the television movie "Net Worth," which said he
died broke in a boxcar.

But he was much, much more than a hard-luck story. Doug
Harvey was at turns indomitable and hopelessly insecure,
self-involved and highly principled. He was ruthless and
overwhelmingly compassionate, a visionary who was nonetheless wholly tragic, the recipient of glorious gifts and
grievous burdens.

It is both easy and tempting to paint Doug Harvey as either
a hopeless drunk or, since he was one of the ringleaders of an
attempted players' union crushed by NHL owners, a martyr in
the battle for the emancipation of exploited hockey players.
He was both, and he was neither. Harvey wore paradox as
proudly as red, white and blue.

In the company of players who shared his time, Doug
Harvey stories fall like the leaves in autumn. Unquestionably

the greatest defenseman of his era, a seven-time Norris Trophy winner, Harvey is still regarded by many as "The Prototype," the perfect blend of offense and defense, the mold from which Larry Robinson, Ray Bourque and even Bobby Orr were minted.

Toe Blake coached against Orr and saw Paul Coffey, but he considered Harvey's the one game above reproach. "As far as I'm concerned, he's far and away the best defenseman ever," Blake said. "You look over all the great defensemen and there was always something they couldn't do. But not Harvey. He does everything."

That Harvey scored only nine goals in his most prolific NHL season says everything about his values and little about his effectiveness. Blake told friends Harvey could score 20 goals at will. He just didn't care to.

Harvey's influence extended far past the potential of a 20-goal season; his control was evident in the nonstatistical, the human and therefore nebulous areas of the game: defense, playmaking, pace and leadership. The only statistic that concerned Harvey was the score and during his tenure, the Canadiens lost only three regular season games out of every ten and won six Stanley Cups.

Harvey grew up in a family of five in Montreal's Notre Dame de Grace area, the son of Alfred Harvey, a clerk for a pharmaceutical company, and his wife, Martha. Alfred Harvey was a devout but humorous man who eschewed cursing, alcohol and tobacco and treated his wife and friends lovingly. Martha was a genial, warm mother and Doug and his two brothers were raised in a stable, loving home.

Athletic as a child, Harvey soon grew into a startling talent.

Barrel-chested with terrific hand speed, he was a good enough ballplayer for major league baseball's Boston Braves to try to sign while Harvey was in his teens. Harvey preferred to stay at home, where he could also play football and hockey, first with the junior Montreal Royals and later, the Quebec Aces.

Harvey joined the merchant marines in 1940 as an 18-year-old, intent on adventure on a cargo freighter. His plans were temporarily derailed when an officer familiar with his baseball ability tried to draft him onto his ship so Harvey could play on his baseball team. "He assigned me to a job called dock messenger so that I couldn't join my ship," Harvey later told an interviewer. "Well, that was the worst mistake he ever made. I kicked up so badly, they were relieved to get rid of me and send me off to my ship. Just because I was good at sports, was that any reason to keep me from doing my business?"

Harvey's defiance of a superior officer was altogether in keeping with the person he was and the man he was becoming. He was uncannily self-possessed and more than willing to challenge authority.

After two years in the service, Harvey was discharged. He put in some time with the Quebec Senior Aces before signing with Montreal when the club offered him $6,000 a season plus a $2,000 bonus. He made the Canadiens in the 1947–48 season and scored four goals and added four assists before being sent to Buffalo in the American League after 35 NHL games for more seasoning.

Harvey was back up for good the following season, but he was nonetheless regarded as a novelty; his athletic ability and good skating skills were obvious but so was a laconic style and a stubborn habit of carrying the puck across his crease.

For the first several years with the Canadiens, those habits made him roundly unpopular with fans, management and media. Typically, the censure made Harvey more determined to flout convention. He would often look toward the Canadiens bench as he slowly crossed the crease with the puck and then comment loudly on the bench about how he had gotten away with it.

It has been 30 years since Doug Harvey played in the NHL, and generations of fans unfamiliar with Harvey's game point to his astounding number of Norris Trophies and assume he bridged the gap between the era of the hulking, stay-at-home defenseman of the 1920s and 1930s and the dashing rushing style Bobby Orr popularized in the 1960s. In a way, he did, but this theory ignores the handful of good rushing defensemen who came before and during Harvey's time. Rearguards like Toronto's King Clancy, Boston's Eddie Shore and Montreal's Kenny Reardon moved the puck out of their own zone with confidence long before Doug Harvey reached the NHL. The Maple Leafs' Hap Day scored 14 times from the blue line nearly 20 years before Harvey's first game. Shore scored 12 goals in his rookie year of 1926–27 and had double digits in each of his next four years; Detroit defenseman Flash Hollett was the game's first 20-goal defenseman two years before Harvey's arrival in the NHL.

But as the game began to evolve in the 1930s, defense-oriented coaches, spearheaded by Toronto's Day, began exerting more and more influence on tactics. In the decade before Harvey, forwards were more or less on their own in the attacking zone against the two opposing defensemen and the opposing line. From a defensive point of view, five men against three made excellent odds and reduced the call for a fast and mobile defenseman to move the puck out of danger. Instead, teams usually opted for big, tough defensemen, typified by the Canadiens' Butch Bouchard and Detroit's Bob Goldham, who could use their great strength and reach to clear the crease and the slot. Most teams carried one defenseman who could be trusted to lug the puck into the opposing zone, but even then, his defensive position would be filled temporarily by a forward who dropped back. The New York Rangers and later, the Toronto Maple Leafs, used Babe Pratt in that role. The Red Wings were blessed with Hollett and later Red Kelly, a Harvey contemporary who scored 15 or more goals for seven consecutive seasons.

But the tinkering of coaches had left the natural flow of the game in shambles. Forwards spent endless shifts trapped in their own end. Defensemen, even those who could rush the puck, were stuck: they were usually either too slow to begin a transition game or simply lacked a target, since all the forwards who could accept a pass were still in the defensemen's end of the rink. Often all the defenseman could manage was to indiscriminately dump the puck out of the zone, where it was easily gathered in by the opposition.

Harvey's genius was in recognizing that, while aesthetically pleasing for the fans and newspaper people, a rushing defenseman, even a great rushing defenseman, was of limited use under the existing framework. So Doug Harvey changed the blueprint by which the game was played. In the process, he became the founding father of Firewagon Hockey. When he finally made the all-star team in 1952, Harvey addressed his critics in a first-person article in *The Hockey News*:

"You know, sometimes you wonder when you take the puck and hear a crowd boo you. You figure maybe they're right and you're wrong. I was tempted to change my style of play once because of that. I never did though. I was going to become the "shoot it out" guy and "the great rusher." That's the best way to make the All-Star team, and make the fans love you. Just keep rushing up the ice. They love it and they think you're playing a heck of a game. When we're up a goal my first thought is to protect the lead. Particularly if time is getting short. I'm not rushing up the ice all night if I can protect a lead by staying back."

Harvey was equally disdainful of the idea of chipping the puck out of harm's way late in the game:

"Often when we're up a goal in the last minutes, I can hear people yelling 'Shoot it out. Get it out of there,'" he wrote. "That's easy to do. I can shoot that puck out of there anytime. I can sit back there and shoot it out when I'm 50 years old if they'll let me. But when that one goal makes the difference, I'm not throwing any pucks away. I'm trying to do what's best for the team that's why I take my time and make the play. Oh, I know I look like I'm playing dangerously when I play around my own net, but that's the way I play the game. I know what I'm doing back there, believe me."

He did indeed. Harvey used the boards creatively and became an early master of banking the puck out of the zone to streaking teammates. He was fantastically poised with the puck, and the spinerama move popularized by Bobby Orr and Serge Savard was a Harvey staple a generation before.

Harvey was virtually impossible to get around. After practice he would offer a bounty to anyone who could move the puck around him. To make it interesting he held his stick by the blade. At 5'11" and 185 pounds, he was big enough to move virtually any forward of his era, fast enough to escape with the puck and smart enough to make a good play when he did. That combination hadn't been seen in the NHL since Eddie Shore's prime in the mid-1930s and Harvey had a more deft passing touch.

"Doug had the soft hands. He could make the play, the pass, he could see the ice," said backup goalie Charlie Hodge who witnessed countless Harvey forays. "That was his forte. He read the play, and he could see the play developing in a way that very few players could."

When, inevitably, Harvey got hold of the puck, opponents feared his passing touch and peeled back. The Canadiens' forwards, secure in the knowledge that Harvey would be beaten very rarely, were afforded the luxury of hanging higher in the defensive zone or even lurking in neutral ice. Harvey's natural skills bought him more room and, unimpeded by forecheckers (Harvey would quickly lose anyone who challenged him), he was free to bring the puck up ice. "He was like a big glider moving with the puck," remembered television analyst Howie Meeker, a veteran of the Harvey era. "He controlled the play so well, his forwards could cheat."

The best remembered image of Doug Harvey is of a slightly stout defenseman coming out from behind the right side of net, slowly leading the Canadiens up ice in an unhurried upright stride. Once across the blue line, he would feather a pass across to the winger on the left side and the Canadiens were once again on the attack. The genesis of headmanning the puck, the style of hockey popularized by the Canadiens and the style of hockey many still feel is the game at its best, came with Doug Harvey's refusal to conform to the convention of the time.

Only two other position players, Wayne Gretzky and Bobby Orr, have altered the game as profoundly as Doug Harvey did. Orr was one of the game's all-time premier skaters and his defensive instincts were as sharp as his ability to sense a scoring chance. The Bruins only scored on a small percentage of his rushes, but Orr was so fast, he could get back into the play after a rush had gone wrong and start the cycle from defense to offense again.

The real similarity between Doug Harvey and Bobby Orr, and the thing that made both so valuable, is that each could grasp the pace of the game and manipulate it to what their team needed, Orr with his speed and puckhandling, Harvey with his positional play and passing.

Glen Sather used the Montreal style of headmanning the puck as a blueprint in assembling the great Edmonton Oiler teams of the 1980s. The linchpin of those teams was Paul Coffey, who, like Harvey, was blessed with a deep cast of premier forwards. Coffey's most noticeable asset, like Orr's, was his formidable rushing skills but it was Coffey's ability to find a streaking Gretzky or Mark Messier and instantly convert defense into offense that powered the Oilers. The nucleus of those teams is scattered throughout the NHL and Harvey's descendants—Coffey, Gretzky, Messier—remain dominant figures in the NHL.

By his fourth season, 1951–52, Harvey had gone from a talented if unconventional background player to a dominating defender. In Detroit, in January of 1952, hockey writer Marshall Dann polled all six NHL coaches for a mid-season all-star team. To the surprise of newspaper people, Harvey accompanied the far better known Red Kelly on every ballot. It was the first benchmark of what would become Harvey's prime, an era that included seven straight first-team all-star selections.

Dangerous at even strength, Harvey was lethal when the Canadiens enjoyed the man advantage. Harvey, who shifted easily from right to left defense, often took the left side on the Canadiens' power play, the better to find Rocket Richard on the right flank. The NHL's move to change the rules in 1956–57 to permit the return of a player assessed a minor penalty after the opponent scored their first power play goal was intended to blunt the Canadiens' fearsome power play and restore more parity to the league.

The stars of the Canadiens' power play orbited around Harvey. "To tell you how great he was," said longtime adversary Ted Lindsay of the Detroit Red Wings, "whenever he was on the ice, he'd have guys like Geoffrion, Beliveau, Moore, Olmstead and the Rocket on the power play. He controlled them. When you can orchestrate a great bunch of talent, that shows leadership."

Harvey won his first Cup with the Canadiens in 1953. Beginning in 1955, he won seven Norris Trophies, emblematic of the league's best defenseman, in eight years. By now, his innate ability to control the game was in full flower. As he entered his thirties, he was physically at his peak and his ability to read the play and willingness to follow his instincts were indomitable.

Once in a playoff game against Boston, the Canadiens were leading by a goal late in the third period. The Bruins' Réal Chevrefils, a good goalscorer, had the puck in the Montreal end and was shifting about in the corner. Harvey stood between him and the net, staring idly at the Boston forward. Chevrefils darted toward Harvey and then jumped back, stick-handled and stayed in the corner. Harvey stood there, one writer reported, as if waiting for a bus. Eventually, one of the Canadiens forwards got back and forced Chevrefils to try to make a play. Chevrefils turned the puck over, Harvey gathered the puck in and started the Canadiens once again up ice. Montreal won the game, and Harvey was asked later why he didn't, as the game's conventions called for at the time, challenge Chevrefils. "What for?" Harvey asked. "He could have stayed there until the end of the game for all I cared. How many guys have you seen score from the corner?"

Players acquired by the Canadiens were quickly introduced to the Harvey way of doing things. "I won't give you the puck if you're not skating," Harvey would tell newly acquired players. "If you're standing still, if you park yourself near the boards and wait for a pass from me, it won't come. You'll die of old age standing at the boards. If you want the puck, you'll get it on the fly."

Harvey's obsession with minimizing effort sometimes made it seem like he was barely trying and it was an image he liked to perpetuate. "I don't think the point is whether or not you're loafing, but whether you know when to loaf," he said of his sometimes laid-back style.

In a blow-out, Harvey was all but invisible. "He used to say, save the goals for tomorrow night," recalled left-winger Dickie Moore. "We'll need some tomorrow night too." "If the game was 8–2," said Hal Laycoe, a defenseman with the Bruins, Canadiens and Rangers, "Doug Harvey might have a goal or an assist. But if it was 3–2, he'd have two or three points."

Off the ice, Harvey's refusal to conform was a nightmare for coaches, managers and even some of his teammates. Rocket Richard was one of several Canadiens aggravated by his perpetual tardiness. If Harvey was on time, it was by the narrowest of margins. "He'd be the last one on the bus, the last one down from the hotel room to take the bus to the airport," remembered Kenny Reardon, a veteran of the Montreal blue line who moved into the front office after his retirement as a player. "It was always 'Where's Doug?' You were waiting, waiting, and if you said, 'Doug, I'll fine you a hundred, I'll fine you fifty,' he didn't give a shit."

For Harvey, life with the Canadiens was a perpetual adolescence. He had adulation and recognition as the game's best defenseman, the company of his peers and a heavy diet of winning. Harvey was the Canadiens' premier problem child, and he attacked life with childlike enthusiasm even after marrying and beginning a family of his own, one which would eventually include six children.

"When you were management, you were continually kept on tenterhooks," said Reardon. "You're going into Toronto and the Grey Cup football game is [also on] on a cold Saturday. The orders are, nobody goes to that football game, we don't want you sitting in that cold all afternoon. You know who would go to the game? Harvey."

"We would play cards, play jokes on the guys, give initiations," Harvey once said. "Sometimes we had to smoke rookies out of their bunks, setting fires and all that. We'd pay the railroad after it was over. One time, it cost us $1,100. No sweat." One of Harvey's favorite pranks was finding out a player's medical information and sprinkling whatever the player was allergic to in his bed.

When gangs, led by Harvey, found themselves short of initiation victims, they would redo a rookie or even take on a veteran. "We grabbed the Rocket when there was nobody else available for the second time," Harvey once recalled. "We shaved every hair off his body. He was so mad, he leaped up and punched me in the mouth and broke a couple of teeth. They had to separate us but the next morning, we had breakfast together. That's how it was in those days."

During an exhibition game in Sudbury against the Ontario Senior Hockey League Wolves, the Canadiens led by 5–0, much to the satisfaction of coach Toe Blake, a Sudbury-area native who was anxious to show he had made good. Then and now, the arena featured a wolf dummy that would circle the rink on a guy wire whenever the home team scored. When the Wolves finally beat Jacques Plante for a goal, the wolf circled the rink and the hometown crowd roared its approval. Harvey was so taken by the stunt that the first chance he got, he shot the puck past a stunned Plante. Blake was furious and when Harvey returned to the bench, "Sorry, Toe," said Harvey, "but seeing that wolf again was worth it."

Belittling Harvey was hopeless, his sense of self-esteem seemed unassailable. In Harvey's early days with the Canadiens, Dick Irvin would attempt to motivate Harvey by berating him, said longtime teammate Bert Olmstead. "That wasn't the way to handle Harvey. I'd shout at him across the dressing room, I wanted him to try harder. I didn't think he was giving it his best shot and he said he was."

Harvey's insolence was viewed as harmful to team unity and Canadiens general manager Frank Selke once forbade Toe Blake to use Harvey on the power play. "This guy thinks he can run this hockey team and we're going to prove to him he can't," Selke told Blake. The Montreal coach obeyed orders and Harvey stayed on the bench when the Canadiens had the man advantage. The Canadiens won, and absolutely nothing was solved.

Every story added to the Harvey lore. He was skilled with his hands and during an off day in the fall, *Montreal Star* reporter Eddie MacCabe was dispatched to see how Harvey was doing on a new house he was building. The house was incomplete; there was little more than a foundation, and rain followed by freezing temperatures had turned the basement into a perfect rink. MacCabe found Doug Harvey the home-building hockey player downstairs, playing shinny in his boots with skate-wearing neighborhood kids.

But what made Harvey so unforgettable to his friends was a generosity as prodigious as his on-ice talents. He gave much of his money away. His oldest son, Doug Junior, recalled his father helping a stranded motorist on a trip to Quebec City.

"I would have been 10 or 11 years old, so he was 35 or so. Around 7:30 in the morning, there's this car parked on the side of the road. Dad pulls in behind him—of course, you could never pass a parked car. Anyway, he starts talking to this couple, they were older, and they were having car problems. They were on their way to a wedding and they had to be there for 11 o'clock in the morning. So Dad says, 'Look, I don't have to be in Quebec City until about 3 in the afternoon. I'll meet you at so and so street, and you can give me my car back.' He never saw these people before, they could have gone to New York for all he knew. Sure enough, he gets the car all fixed for them, the water pump was gone or something. So he pays the bill, meets these guys at 5 o'clock in Quebec City. They thank him very much, he won't take the money for repairing their car. Off we went. He did stuff like that all the time."

Dickie Moore remembered an incident before an exhibition game in Vancouver. The team was eating in a posh meeting room when a shoddily dressed man entered, asking for Doug Harvey. The man was a former player who was obviously living on the street. Harvey put his arm around the man, led him to his table, sat beside him and instructed the waiter to bring him anything he wanted. When it was time to go, Harvey shook the player's hand and slipped some money in his pocket. Many people will give to the needy, few will consort with them and treat them as equals.

Every member of the Canadiens knew they had a friend in Harvey. "Even when Rocket was captain, when, as a young player, you needed something," said Jean Beliveau, "you went to Doug Harvey."

"He always left you feeling that your time was his time," said Howard Riopelle, a Harvey teammate in Montreal and a friend for nearly 50 years. "No matter how much of a hurry he was in, he felt your time was more valuable and he spoke to you, even at the expense of maybe being a little late. He loved people."

If Harvey's kindness kept him surrounded by friends, his on-ice skills and crunch-time toughness kept him employed. "Everybody loves a rebel," noted Reardon. "And he was a rebel who could outplay the other guy too. As a player, you've got to admire a guy like that."

As he aged, Harvey's antics became more difficult to understand. It took effort to be so consistently late and the money he lavished on strangers would have been far wiser spent on his family. "Doug Harvey," said Canadiens' backup goalie Charlie Hodge, "was good to everyone but himself and his family."

His confidence was superhuman. The first time Harvey curled he got into an argument with Bert Olmstead and Toe Blake, who had curled almost all their lives, because he wanted to be the skip. What no one knew is that Harvey's increasingly erratic behavior fit what is now understood as a familiar pattern. Doug Harvey suffered from bipolar disorder; he was a manic-depressive and was diagnosed as such late in his life when his body was too devastated by years of alcohol use to accommodate any medication. It wouldn't have mattered: he refused to accept the diagnosis and by the end of his life, the tandem of alcoholism and bipolar disorder were hopelessly intermingled. "It was something we didn't realize until much later," said Doug Harvey, Jr., "By then, it was very late in my dad's life."

Bipolar disease is often linked to creative, gifted personalities whose moods go back and forth between absolute confidence and a fear so profound they can hardly get out of bed. At home, Harvey was by turns overwhelmingly energetic or terribly quiet and he disavowed any consistent responsibility in raising his children. The real curse of the disease is that while the depression stage of the bipolar's mood swing is horrifically painful, the person who suffers from the disease often does more real harm when he or she is manic.

People with bipolar disease are often spectacularly generous and loving to strangers and casual friends. They are frequently terrible with money, because their rush of confidence is so overwhelming, they see no repercussions to their spending sprees. Alcohol and drug use is endemic to the disease. With no real psychic middle ground on which to live, sobriety inevitably means an eventual return to the pain of depression, which is habitually warded off with drink or drugs.

Harvey's flippant attitude toward his superiors masked a fierce and desperate competitiveness. He never talked to opponents, and while this was the norm of the era, he took it to extraordinary lengths. Win or lose, he never shook hands with the opposition after a playoff series. "My whole life has been sort of a war," he said in 1973. "Every game I played, I treated them like a battle. Hockey particularly, because that was my bread and butter. I can't understand how players can be palsy-walsy with each other."

On one occasion, Toe Blake, wanting to limit the nocturnal wanderings of Harvey and some of the other Canadiens, scheduled an early-morning tour of a Michigan auto plant the day after a game against Detroit. Harvey was aghast and defied Blake by walking off the bus when he learned some Red Wings would be accompanying the Canadiens.

Harvey almost killed the Rangers Red Sullivan with a vicious spear. Sullivan underwent surgery for a ruptured spleen and received the last rites of the Catholic Church. He played again, but only after a lengthy convalescence. "Sure I speared him," Harvey said when asked after the game. "He was kicking skates. He did it three times the game before and I warned him. Then he did it again, so I got him."

Harvey loved to play so much that the end of the season triggered an annual funk, even during the six Stanley Cup winning years. "I'd go into a terrible depression, for three or four days after the season ended," he once told newspaperman Tim Burke. "Other guys would come to the Forum to collect their stuff and say they didn't want to see skates or sticks for six months. Know what I'd do? I'd put on the skates and go out and fool around for hours for a few days after the season. Finally, I'd get over it and go out and play ball or something."

His disease made Harvey at turns inappropriately cocky and terribly insecure about his position with the Canadiens. Petrified of losing his spot in the lineup, he played with all ranges of injuries. Harvey appeared in 94 percent of the regular season games for which he was eligible and once played 51 straight games with a cracked ankle because the Canadiens were down to only three serviceable defenseman.

"You don't think I'm going to take any chances on being out of the lineup," he told the *Toronto Star*'s Milt Dunnell in 1960. "Three years ago, Jean Beliveau was out for a few games. He came back and was ready to play. Believe it or not, the club was going so well, Jean couldn't break in. He didn't have a regular position for seven or eight games. We told him we'd keep on winning and he'd sit out all season. If that could happen to Beliveau, you think it couldn't happen to me?"

When Rocket Richard retired at the end of the 1959–60 season, Harvey was elected the Canadiens' new captain. Clearly, the Canadiens management would have preferred

Beliveau for the job but the players' vote made that impossible. Harvey was an excellent leader; he liked the idea of being captain, just the way he liked the notion of being the skip on his maiden voyage in curling. However, he was profoundly ill-suited for the captaincy. Being captain demanded an even hand and a heaping measure of diplomacy when dealing with the club and media. It meant understanding and implementing compromise, a concept Harvey could not grasp when he was depressed and had no time for when he was manic.

His shortcomings became even more glaring when Montreal's five-year championship reign fell in Harvey's first and only year with the "C." The Canadiens were in an untenable position. Harvey's behavior was growing more and more bellicose by the year and his drinking was beginning to alarm management. Before the year began, some club officials warned him it could lead to a trade. Harvey ignored it, as he did most warnings.

Also galling to the Canadiens' front office was Harvey's involvement in the formation of a short-lived players' association. Harvey found the idea of a union abhorrent but, like many across the league, he was unhappy about the heavy-handed way in which ownership dominated players. Owners often traded and demoted players callously and the idea of a player agent, had it been broached, would have been considered beyond belief. Players could, and often did, hold out but in the main, they took what they were offered or they did not play. Yet any study of the league's finances would explode the carefully nurtured public perception that the NHL was financially fragile and therefore would have been unable to survive larger player salaries.

Another example of the owner's impunity was the NHL pension plan, instituted in 1947. Players could, and often did, deposit as much as $900 per season. But despite those contributions, players were given scant if any access to financial information on how the money was being managed. And, while the pension fund was to receive two-thirds of the proceeds from every all-star game, management, entrusted with working the box office, invariably reported receipts that were less than a third of what the players thought they should be.

Always obstinate, Harvey was particularly unyielding on questions of principle. He thought the clause that bound players at the club's option was unfair and he scratched it out of his contracts. The Canadiens, knowing Harvey wanted nothing but to play in Montreal and mindful that none of their league lodge brothers would attempt to sign Harvey and prompt a bidding war, let him have his way.

Bill Dineen, an opponent in Detroit and an eventual co-manager with Harvey of the WHA's Houston Aeros, said Harvey was a compulsively moral man. What mattered most, was what Harvey himself called "The Code." Red Sullivan broke it when he kicked skates; NHL owners were breaking it by mistreating players. "He had his code, he had his ethics and what he thought was right and wrong," said Dineen. "Boy, if everybody lived by that, the world would be a better place. The whole code was based on fairness. He was very fair; monetary things didn't really mean anything to him but he didn't want anybody taking advantage of anybody."

Ted Lindsay and Harvey, the players' representatives on a five-person player-management board, soon tired of what they viewed as the owners' attempts at stonewalling. Despite an on-ice history of absolute brutality toward each other, they began working to stitch together the idea of a player union. "It seemed totally against the spirit of the game," Harvey would say later, "and it turned out the hardest thing I had to do in hockey was associating with Lindsay at a pension-plan meeting."

"We never talked because we hated each other," Lindsay said recently. "But you knew what was going on and you had a purpose. You're an adult, you've got a brain." When NHL president Clarence Campbell told them the Maple Leafs' president Conn Smythe was undertaking an independent audit of the players pension fund and that the players would not have the right to look at it, Harvey and Lindsay were moved to action. Every player but one, Toronto captain Ted Kennedy, agreed to join the union.

Reardon spent hours trying to talk Harvey out of an association and arranged a meeting between the club, Frank Selke and owner Senator Hartland Molson. "That meeting was the beginning of the breaking away of the union of the Montreal Canadiens. The whole thing was a vendetta by the players aimed at Conn Smythe and (Detroit Red Wings' GM) Jack Adams," Reardon said. "We had these trumped-up ideas about how other guys were getting screwed, but not our team. We would stick with the other guys if they could beat Adams and Smythe."

Adams convinced Red Kelly and Gordie Howe to leave the association. In the summer of 1957, in a clear signal that union activism would be punished, the Red Wings traded Lindsay, their perennial all-star left-winger, to Chicago. After harassing and abusing him, Smythe sent Jimmy Thomson, a ten-year veteran and a superb defender from Toronto to Chicago, where he lasted one season before retiring. The proposed union collapsed and a quiet countdown began on how long Harvey would last.

In the summer of 1961, the Canadiens traded Doug Harvey, then 36 and the reigning Norris Trophy winner, to the New York Rangers. Despite the four-year time lag, several Canadiens were sure Harvey's trade to the Rangers, a perennial sad sack, was punishment for his union activities. "Doug stuck his neck out," said Dickie Moore. "He said we're not here to strike, not here to hurt the owners. We just want some information. Eventually, they found a way to get rid of him."

The timing of the trade, however, augers heavily against the theory that like Lindsay and Thomson, Harvey was banished for his role in the union. It had, after all, been four years since the union was broken and while they were not always model employers, the Canadiens operated with a level of pragmatism that precluded trading a player because he spoke of a union.

"Our team wasn't vindictive; we were never stupid enough to send good players away for nothing," Reardon said. The trade, he said, was necessitated by Harvey's age and his constant challenges to authority. Soon the combination of advancing years and lifestyle would catch up with Harvey and while a dignified retirement with the Canadiens might be the reward for a good company man, Harvey had made plenty of enemies in management.

"It had just gotten to the point where we could hardly handle him. I mean he was every fan's idol and management's curse," said Reardon. "Rules weren't for him. Doug Harvey could run everything but himself."

Reardon, the Canadiens' assistant general manager, had spent much of the summer trying to figure out how to allocate his 18 spots on the major league roster and avoid losing promising young players through the waiver draft. He was toying with the idea of urging his boss, Frank Selke, to drop Harvey altogether but knew that kind of a move would be construed as a horrible slap to a well-loved and much-honored contributor. Then one day, providence arrived by telephone in the shape of New York Rangers' general manager Muzz Patrick.

"Muzz said, 'If I could get one good player like Harvey as a coach and a player, that would really hold my club together,'" Reardon recalled. "I know Selke is unhappy with Harvey, we're just at the point of unloading him and we don't know how to unload him. It's very hard not to protect your captain. Muzz said 'If I got him, maybe I'd make him player coach.' I said, here's our chance, we're going to unload him and elevate him at the same time."

"I said, 'Wait, I'll talk to Mr. Selke' and I put the phone down, got up from my desk and stamped the floor, pretending that I was going down the corridor to Selke's office. I came back and said, 'Mr. Selke's interested, provided he's your coach.' That's how it started."

The departure from Montreal has been pinned as one of the central turning points in Doug Harvey's life, since he clearly began to disintegrate a year or two after leaving the Canadiens. In truth, his disease was already beginning to erode his personality. He began spending long periods of time in the off-season in bed and to some, his manner seemed to harden toward his teammates.

"As the years went by, Doug changed," Maurice Richard wrote in his book, *The Flying Frenchmen*. "Toward the end of his career in Montreal, he became too direct in his criticism of the various players and began getting the others angry at him so that his effectiveness in the dressing room was lost."

Harvey was bitter about the trade, but it was an anger that he would feel much more keenly later in his life. Arriving in New York with his family as player-coach, Harvey immediately became one of the brightest lights of Broadway. The Rangers, shut out of the playoffs the previous three seasons made the post-season and dropped their goals against by nearly half a goal a game. New York lost the semi-final in six games, extending the eventual Stanley Cup champion Maple Leafs to four one-goal victories.

"He came to New York in the best shape of his life," said Harry Howell, Harvey's defense partner that year and a Hall-of-Fame Rangers' defenseman. "He had a terrific year and I really appreciated playing with the guy because he knew everything there was to know about playing defense. Playing one season with Doug Harvey was like playing ten years with someone else."

Harvey cut back his drinking dramatically in New York. But coaching meant that he had to keep his distance from the players and for the first time, Harvey felt lonely within the game.

While observers talked openly of Harvey succeeding Patrick when his on-ice career ended in a year or two, Harvey was unwilling to let his playing adolescence slip away. Before the 1962 training camp, he told the Rangers' upper management that although it meant a pay cut of $7,500—from $27,500 to $20,000—he wanted to return strictly as a player. Reinstated as a full-time player, Harvey sent his family back to Montreal and began to drink heavily again.

Teammates say that alcohol did not affect Harvey's play with the Canadiens and the record book bears out that assertion. Harvey played for 14 years in Montreal and he could not have been the player he was had he been constantly drunk. During those years, "Doug liked a good time," said Olmstead, "but when there was money on the line, it was nutcracking time."

But alcohol clearly was a major factor in his decision to return to the Rangers as a player. Being out with the boys and having a good time meant drinking and long before anyone coined the phrase "substance abuse," beer had been synonymous with sports. Men who would not speak, or at least not candidly, became different, more approachable, at closing time and the links forged over a bar table were still there when the game was played the next night.

"We looked at beer as a release," said Olmstead. "After everything, it was a way to unwind with each other. Nobody was allowed to drink with us. We'd drink a six-pack, get dizzy as a fart and talk about hockey. That's where we got to understand each other. It was the truth serum."

Those circumstances made moderate men more likely to drink and for Harvey, drinking went far past basking in the security of the group. Unaware of his illness, alcohol was also the only real weapon he could use to ward off his increasingly debilitating depression, and he was unapologetic about his love of drinking. "When they drop this body into the ground," he once said, "it won't rot for a long time. It's full of Alcool (an unflavored alcohol). It's got its own embalming fluid."

"He had the worst kind of alcoholism in my opinion," said Howard Riopelle. "He'd say lookit, I'm not going to have a drink for a month and he wouldn't. Then he'd go for a long, long time."

New York should have provided Harvey with the perfect stepping off point from his athletic adolescence. There were no cronies to drag him out, no hard-living image to live up to. He could retire gracefully and move into a front-office job commensurate with his talents and contribution to the game. Harvey's gut feeling for when a player was on the downslide proved unfailing. He told friends two years before Guy Lafleur's burn-out and retirement that the Canadiens' great had lost his will to play. Always anxious to teach, he served as an unofficial coach in every city he played in.

But playing meant more than just being on the ice three hours every second day. It meant traveling, keeping the company of men and living free of commitments. It was a life he felt compelled to live. Long after he dropped out of hockey, Harvey lived a hockey player's life: trips and junkets occupied much of the winter. "Later in his life, it was the same as if he was playing hockey," recalled Doug Harvey, Jr. "He'd be gone five or six months and then be back for several months in the summer."

"He had such a great hockey mind, there's no doubt he could have been a coach or a general manager for years and years," said Bill Dineen. "He was a very brilliant, brilliant person. But, he just had a thing in him, he enjoyed life so much, he felt like he had to be around people in the bar, have a few drinks and associate with people. Anyplace he ever went, he was like the Pied Piper, the kids followed him, everybody followed him."

With or without the captain's C, Harvey wanted to lead and in his frequent confident moods, he seized leadership. But he could not lead every day; the increasing grip of his disease would not allow it. Tom Johnson, a longtime teammate, summed up the apparent dichotomy of Harvey's character perfectly when he said Harvey "wanted to look after 18 players but he didn't want to be their boss. He wanted to be the leader, but not their boss."

Harvey's game slid dramatically as soon as he gave up the coaching duties and the Doug Harvey who started his second year in New York bore no resemblance to the previous year's Norris Trophy winner. "Going back to being a player was the worst thing he ever did because he went back to his old ways," said Howell. "In two months he made up for what he had missed the year before."

By November of 1963, the Rangers decided he was a liability in the lineup. The club offered him the choice of coaching their Baltimore affiliate and staying in shape for a possible return while keeping his NHL salary or his unconditional release. Harvey quit outright.

"It's the first time in NHL history," said Muzz Patrick, "that a player of Doug's stature has been given his unconditional release. The Rocket and Lindsay were frozen on the voluntarily retired list. They couldn't play anywhere else."

The departure from New York triggered a six-year odyssey through the minor leagues in Baltimore, St. Paul, Quebec City, Pittsburgh and Kansas City, while his family stayed in

Montreal. The pay sagged with the caliber of the leagues he frequented. The game Harvey had once controlled so effortlessly now seemed to control him.

"I started at the bottom and worked my way to the top," Harvey told Mike Corbett, a teammate in Baltimore. "I love the game so much, I'll finish at the bottom again."

Harvey popped up with the Detroit Red Wings in 1966–67 and then seemed set to disappear again. But in the 1968 playoffs, Scotty Bowman's St. Louis Blues lost Game Six of their first-round series against Philadelphia, as well as several defensemen to injury. Harvey was player-coach of the Blues' Kansas City affiliate and when Bowman summoned Harvey and a couple more call-ups, Harvey commandeered Dickie Moore's car and drove overnight to Philadelphia. The car broke down on the Interstate and Harvey and the others had to hitchhike the final leg to the arena. He showed up at practice unshaven with his skates hitched over his stick. The Blues won Game Seven 3–1 with Harvey taking a regular turn at 44.

The next season, he played 70 games and savored the irony of being the league's oldest player. "It's like they always say," he told a newspaperman. "You live the good life, you look after the old body and you can go a long time."

Before the playoffs, when it became apparent that Harvey was too old to perform in the post-season, Blues' owner Sid Salomon offered him a job coaching under Bowman. Harvey turned him down, and returned to Kansas City. "Ah, Sid, don't you know," he told Salomon, "I love playing." Later, he admitted he was devastated when the Blues didn't call back. "I was never told that I was through. They just didn't invite me back to training camp. I was lost," he told a friend.

After 19 NHL seasons, Harvey's career as a player had ground to a halt and the pattern of his life became more erratic. In 1970, he was arrested at Ottawa Airport when a search of his baggage revealed a loaded .357 magnum. Harvey, who had his pilot's licence, had flown to Ottawa with some Montreal friends for Chinese food. Police said he attracted attention when he performed an assortment of calisthenics, including handstands, at 4:30 in the morning in the terminal.

One time, he flew his friend Eddie MacCabe from Montreal to Ottawa in a borrowed plane. Harvey eschewed any instrumentation and told MacCabe he would navigate by following the St. Lawrence River. "But you can't see the river because of the cloud cover," MacCabe said. "Jesus, Eddie," answered Harvey. "What do you want to do, look at it all day?"

The arrival of the World Hockey Association in 1973 gave Harvey more bridges into the game. He and Dineen shared the running of the Houston Aeros and Harvey, who had temporarily stopped drinking, was an immediate hit.

"The first year in Houston, we had a luncheon at the arena for all the prominent businessmen, presidents of banks, that sort of thing," Dineen recalled. "They came to me and said 'Bill, somebody's got to talk to these people and tell them about hockey.' I mean they were five rows deep in the stands. So Doug got up there and he had them spellbound, just rolling in the seats. He said, 'You're very proud, rich people, very successful and as far as athletes go, Texas has great football. But you guys are nothing but a bunch of dumb Texans because you know fuck all about hockey.' These were the most prominent people in the city. They talked about him for months after that."

Harvey was almost as unconventional in the front office as he had been on the ice. It was Harvey and Dineen who hatched the plan to draw Gordie Howe back from an unhappy retirement by drafting his son Mark with the club's first choice in the WHA draft. Harvey sealed the deal to procure Mark, Marty and Gordie in a weekend spent playing cribbage with Gordie at the Howe retreat in northern Michigan. Harvey tried to woo Henri Richard to Houston, triggering a bidding war with Montreal that gave Richard an enormous raise.

But nothing seemed to stick. As a scout, Harvey eschewed written reports, and would often describe a prospect's movements on the ice while omitting his name. It fell to Dineen to contact the club and try to figure out who the player was. "He didn't like the night in, night out type of thing," said Dineen. "We paid him but he didn't really work the following year."

In a final snub, the NHL's Hall of Fame selection committee opted to waive the three-year waiting period for Howe and Jean Beliveau but did not nominate Harvey. "It must be a great honor," Howe said at his induction, "if a player like Doug Harvey can't make it." When Harvey was elected the following year (1974) he boycotted the ceremony. The Canadiens, recognizing Harvey's selection for the Hall, retired his number 2 nonetheless.

Harvey opened a restaurant in Montreal, Chez Doug Harvey, but it closed amidst charges that a partner had fled with the proceeds. He refused to claim personal bankruptcy, and instead sold cars for Dickie Moore. He worked selling aluminum windows too, but sloppy bookkeeping meant customers who ordered windows often weren't called back. Predictably, the money which had seemed so plentiful as a player had all but dried up.

By his late fifties, Harvey's life consisted largely of drinking in Montreal taverns or going on extended road trips with friends. He no longer lived with his wife, Ursula and his behavior grew steadily more bizarre. Harvey appeared at a Canadiens game commemorating the team's greatest stars in 1974 dressed in raggedy jeans and wandered absently about. The Forum crowd, which roared at Harvey's introduction, fell quiet when witnessing the depth of his fall.

Finally, in the late 1980s, Tommy Gorman, then living in Ottawa, sent for him in Montreal. "The reason he came up to work for me and stayed with me is my wife and I found Doug and said, you've got to get the hell out of Montreal. You can't go to the tavern down the street and stay there for the day. That's no good for you. Come on up here and work for me." Gorman owned Connaught Race Track in Aylmer, Quebec, 15 minutes away from Ottawa, and Harvey toiled there as a watchman and carpenter. He lived in a railway car on the grounds but the car, once John Diefenbaker's mobile headquarters, was homey and comfortable. The children, with their father's consent, sold the family's Montreal home so Ursula, who endured real financial hardship late in Doug's life, was taken care of.

By now, a lifetime of drinking had hobbled a once-splendid body and it seemed clear that Harvey would not live a long life. (Friends say he drank rarely, if at all, during his last three years.) Gorman approached Montreal president Ronald Corey about a scouting job for Harvey, something that would restore him to the Canadiens' fold and heal the rift that had existed since his trade. Corey, who recognized the value of re-establishing the lustre built by past greats, put Harvey on the payroll as an Ottawa-area scout. The reconciliation thrilled Harvey's friends. "I'll always be proud of the Montreal Canadiens for hiring Doug Harvey again," Moore said. "I'll never forget that."

Harvey spent most of his final year in a Montreal hospital and his stay was underwritten by the Canadiens. Cirrhosis had damaged his body so profoundly that tubes were needed to drain fluids from his stomach and he lost about 40 pounds. One day, Harvey snuck out of hospital to take his grandson to a Canadiens practice. A photographer snapped a shot of an unrecognizable former icon, a gaunt, dying man named Doug Harvey.

Canadiens' coach Pat Burns gathered his players at center ice and nodded discreetly toward Harvey. "If you find that you have problems and your injuries hurt, look over there," said Burns. "That's Doug Harvey, one of the greatest players in the history of the game."

To some, the original estrangement from the Canadiens set the stage for Harvey's drinking. "I think the thing that hurt him was when they traded him from Montreal," Riopelle said. "I think that was the beginning of it because it really hurt his pride. At times he talked about it, but he had an inner secrecy about himself too." "If the Canadiens had treated him right, none of that would have happened," said Gorman.

Others disagreed. "I don't think leaving the Canadiens caused his lifestyle," said Eddie MacCabe, the newspaper buddy who knew Harvey through most of his life. "He was going to be his own man, whether he was a member of the

Montreal Canadiens or the Royal Family, it wouldn't have mattered."

Harvey died on December 26, 1989, one week after his 65th birthday. His funeral, held in the greystone Trinity Memorial Anglican Church in the west-end Notre Dame de Grace neighborhood in which he grew up, was attended by 700 people. Strong men, Jean Beliveau and Henri Richard, wept at the funeral, not so much for a lost talent or friend, but a lost and very gentle soul.

To the world, Doug Harvey died largely by his own hand, the hand that grasped countless bottles and glasses. But in the years since his death, a growing awareness of the virulence of alcoholism has prompted society to view alcoholics more as victims than victimizers. Harvey had an even heavier curse, a mental disease that made alcohol the only socially acceptable anesthetic, and one which carried even more stigma than drinking. The very brilliance that inspired Doug Harvey to change the game had destroyed most elements of his life. He burned too brightly.

At the end, all that was left for Doug Harvey was to play the part of the undaunted individualist. As always, he played it well. Dineen saw him in hospital, ten days before his death and said Harvey was constantly visiting other patients, teasing and kibitzing as if he were back in the Canadiens' dressing room. "If anybody was down, he would make a point of spending time with them and talking with them and bringing them around. He was so good for the morale there, it was unbelievable."

"I remember," Dickie Moore said, speaking of his treasured friend, "He told me, 'Dickie, if I had to do it over again, I'd do it exactly the same way. That's the way he was.'"

But if his friends remember him as stout and uncontrite to the end, he was often sad and sorrowful. Scott Russell, now a "Hockey Night in Canada" host, was working at a Montreal radio station when a rumor began circulating that Harvey was dead. Russell called the hospital and Harvey called back later, crying about the fact that he had to return a phone call to remind the world that he was still alive. Just a few days before his father's death, Doug Harvey, Jr., was walking him back to his hospital bed when Harvey stopped in front of a full-length mirror. "My God," said Doug Harvey. "Look at me."

CHAPTER 5

JEAN BELIVEAU

CAPTAIN 1961–1971

CHAPTER 5

JEAN BELIVEAU

CAPTAIN 1961–1971

Last June 10, as Colorado Avalanche captain Joe Sakic paraded the Stanley Cup around the ice of the Miami Arena, "Hockey Night in Canada" analyst Harry Neale trotted out a Walt Whitman quote he had been saving for years. "O Captain! My Captain!" Neale told his audience. "Our fearful trip is done. Our ship has weathered every rack. The prize we sought is won."

"I would say," Neale said a week later, "that if you had a shot of Jean Beliveau with the Cup it would have been a perfect quote for that occasion too. Jean and Walt, two of a kind. Best at their trade." Jean Beliveau's play and Walt Whitman's writing share a common illusion: the greater the skill of the artist, the more effortless appears the making of the art.

Through the 1950s and 60s, the NHL's standard of elegance was swathed in red, white and blue, was rooted in Montreal and for a decade, wore two Cs. Perhaps only Mario Lemieux, the modern-day player with whom Jean Beliveau is compared most frequently, has ever moved with such prodigious grace. There have been bigger players, but none with the reach, both on the ice and off, of the 6'3", 205-pound Beliveau; faster players, but none with a more far-reaching stride; more charismatic players, but none who have earned a deeper and more lasting respect. And none who so ably defined the model of what a captain should be.

Beliveau is the royalty of hockey captains; he wore the C like a king wore his crown, but while the king's lineage entitles him to the throne, Jean Beliveau made himself a royal. That, more than the goals and assists, even more than his ten Stanley Cups, is the greatest feat of his illustrious career. He made it look easy. To assume that it was easy or that Jean Beliveau's life has been a series of happy confluences would be a mistake. Many who recognized his limitless gifts wondered why he never scored 50 goals, or retired as the game's top goalscorer.

"It's tougher, you're bigger, they're expecting more from you," said Frank Mahovlich, a former Beliveau teammate and himself a survivor of grandiose public expectations. "It wasn't easy for Jean, he worked hard too. I played with him and I know, he worked hard in practice and in preparing himself."

Jean Beliveau's story is about industry, and in his case, its lifelong partners, grace and the illusion of ease. But the man himself knows the truth. "I never thought that my life was easy because I would put my agenda of the last 45 years against anybody's," Beliveau said. "I think I've worked hard all along and I've always tried to be there whenever the team, the company or my family have needed me."

Jean Beliveau was born without the privilege that his grandchildren take for granted. He saw death as a child when his young sister was killed in a car accident. Beliveau was ten in 1939 when his four-year-old sister Helene, was hit by a car in front of the family house. "It was a tragic thing," Beliveau recalled. "I heard the car braking, we were in the backyard. We came running in front of the house and she was lying on the sidewalk like a poor cat or a poor animal. Somebody picked her up and carried her to the neighbor. A doctor came and declared that she was dead."

Beliveau remembers a child's confusion over his sister's death. Only in retrospect would he understand the loss. "You are under the shock," he recalled. "You're young and you have no experience from one thing to the other." As an adult, he lost both parents before his fiftieth birthday. Now, as a greying man, he is helping his daughter and grandchildren to cope with the suicide of their husband and father.

As successful in the boardroom as on the ice, Beliveau has sat on as many as eight boards at once, and emerged as the most untarnished public spokesman hockey has ever known. He was among the first athletes to set up a charitable founda-tion in his name and during his hockey career Beliveau has raised more than $1.5 million for disabled children.

One of the most frequently interviewed men in sports, Beliveau nevertheless retains an aura uneroded by media exposure. Every question posed to him is answered thoroughly and patiently, as if for the first time. Behind the regal countenance and still-majestic features beats the heart of a small-town boy whose father worked for the power company.

"When I accept something, I've always said do it right," said Jean Beliveau, speaking by phone from home. "Take the time. Too often you go to an event, you see athletes or personalities who look at their watch wondering when is this thing going to be over. Maybe one of my secrets is to give the organization or the person more than they were expecting."

Jean Beliveau blossomed late; while he spent much of his winters on the hockey rink he did not play organized hockey until he was 12. The son of Arthur, a hydro-electrical plant employee, and Laurette Beliveau, he grew up in working-class Victoriaville. The Beliveaus were staunchly Catholic. Jean, the eldest of eight children, subscribed to the small-town values of the day. In his book, Jean Beliveau, *My Life in Hockey*, Beliveau recalled his father's value system, the same one he operates from today. "My dad used to say, Jean, no matter how people will approach you with money and gifts and offers that seem ridiculously easy, you must remember that nothing comes free in this life and that hard work and discipline will make you who and what you are."

Beliveau played outdoor pickup hockey from November to March, but stepped into organized play with the Brothers of the Sacred Heart at L'Academie in Victoriaville and the Inter-mediate B Victoriaville Panthers. He also was an excellent baseball player, and at the age of 15, Beliveau became a sum-mer employee of the mining town of Val d'Or so he could be a regular on the town's baseball team. A major league base-ball bird dog was among the first to notice his obvious athletic ability, but Laurette Beliveau forbade her son from signing a minor league contract that would have sent him to the Ameri-can south at such a tender age.

By his mid-teens, the lineup of suitors anxious to exploit Beliveau's hockey talents seemed to be growing by the day. Beliveau was invited to play for the Trois-Rivières Reds of

The Stanley Cup finds a home for the eighth and final time in the arms of Maurice Richard in 1960, as Clarence Campbell looks on. In Game Three of the series, Richard scored his 34th and last goal in the Stanley Cup final and that mark remains the standard today. *Imperial Oil—Turofsky/Hockey Hall of Fame*

In the late 1940s and early 1950s, any action near the Canadiens net invariably involved captain Butch Bouchard, here defending against Leafs left-winger Sid Smith. Bouchard anchored the blue line for 15 seasons and played with four Cup winners. *Imperial Oil—Turofsky/Hockey Hall of Fame*

A leader long before he became a coach, Canadiens' captain Toe Blake unwinds with the Rocket moments after a game. The two were a superb pairing, both as linemates and as a coach and player tandem. *Imperial Oil— Turofsky/Hockey Hall of Fame*

The Punch line. Maurice Richard on right-wing, Elmer Lach at center and Toe Blake on left-wing were rivalled only by Detroit's Production Line as the pre-eminent unit in the 1940s NHL. "Maurice," said Lach, "could put the puck through the eye of a needle," but the line also depended on Lach's playmaking and Blake's tenacious two-way game. *Imperial Oil— Turofsky/Hockey Hall of Fame*

Eyes blackened by a broken nose, Bruins' goaltender Sugar Jim Henry shakes the hand
of a dazed and bleeding Maurice Richard after the Rocket scored to beat the Bruins in
Game Seven of the 1952 semi-final. Richard had left the game in the second with a
severe concussion, and had scored the winner, some think, in a semi-conscious state.
Montreal Gazette

Doug Harvey is about to clear the puck out of harm's way while teammates Claude Provost and Bert Marshall look on. Considered by many to be the greatest all-around defenseman ever to play, Harvey succeeded Maurice Richard as captain in 1960, but he was traded the following year. *Imperial Oil—Turofsky/Hockey Hall of Fame*

Wearing the two "C"s that would become his personal trademarks, the familiar Canadiens "C" as well as the one that denotes the captaincy, Jean Beliveau strikes a casual pose. *Denis Brodeur*

The 1960s belonged to the Montreal Canadiens and their captain, Jean Beliveau. The Canadiens went to the finals six times during the decade and won five Cups. Beliveau's 12 goals in the Stanley Cup final were more than any player had in the decade. *Denis Brodeur*

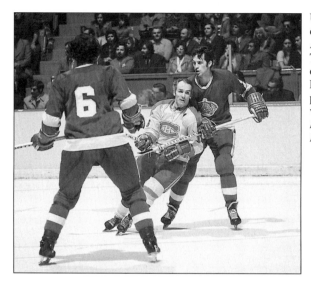

Undersized against opponents like Los Angeles defenseman Terry Harper, but never outworked, Henri Richard fights his way past a stick check to veer in on goal. *Frank Prazak/Hockey Hall of Fame*

Henri Richard with his personal trophy, the Stanley Cup. Richard won the Cup an incredible 11 times, more than any other player. This championship, earned in 1971, was among the sweetest as Richard, benched earlier in the series, scored the tying and winning goals as the Canadiens upset a powerhouse Chicago Blackhawks team with a 3–2 victory in Game Seven. *Denis Brodeur*

Yvan Cournoyer readies for the puck in a 1976 road game. Cournoyer was 31 when his teammates voted him the "C" and the Canadiens won the Stanley Cup in four of the five years in which he wore it. *Bruce Bennett Studios*

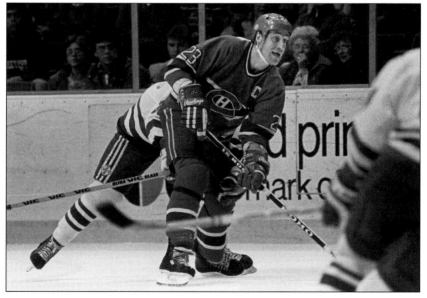

Bob Gainey, of whom teammate Doug Risebrough said, "He always walked the great line [between] being a friend when a player needed it and kicking some players in the ass when they weren't living up to their obligations as teammates." *Bruce Bennett Studios*

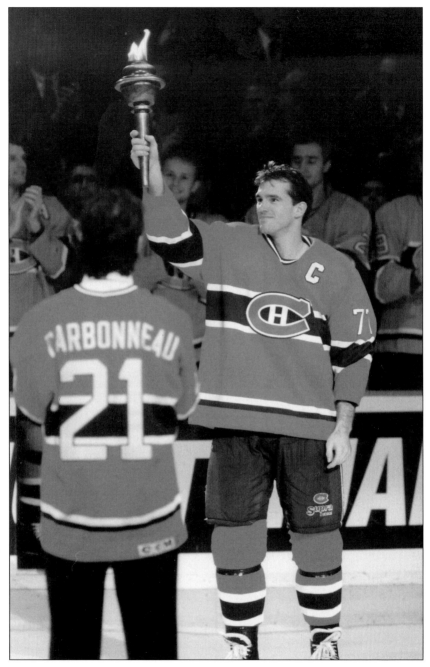

Long a symbol of leadership and loyalty to the Canadiens franchise, the torch is raised by Pierre Turgeon at the closing of the Montreal Forum, March 11, 1996. Turgeon is the 22nd Canadien to wear the "C". *Bruce Bennett Studios*

the Quebec Junior A league at 16 but his father vetoed the move, saying that his son was still too young to leave home. That season, playing in a Victoriaville intermediate league open to players regardless of age, Beliveau scored 47 goals and added 21 assists.

In 1946, Frank Selke arrived in Montreal and immediately set about professionalizing the Canadiens' farm system. Word quickly reached him about a magnificent prospect in Victoriaville and one Saturday, a Canadiens scout named Mickey Hennessey stopped Beliveau on his way home from a baseball game. Hennessey took Beliveau to a lunch counter, piled up $200 in $10 bills and tried to induce him to sign a C form that would have committed him to the Canadiens. "When you have a quarter in your pocket, yes it got my attention," Beliveau recalled. "But my father said no."

Sidetracking money-bearing scouts would become a familiar practice for Arthur Beliveau, who saw no fairness in the system of the day, which permanently indentured a player to one team upon signing. Instead, adamant that Jean retain control of his own future, he advised him to sign with the Junior Victoriaville Tigres for the 1948–49 season, with a legal caveat that Jean would be a free agent after the season. "In the spring," Arthur told the hockey men, "my boy belongs to me."

After dominating the season in Victoriaville, it became clear that Beliveau's talents were too big for the forum into which he had been born. Beliveau signed a one-year contract with the Quebec Junior league's Quebec Citadels in 1949–50 and began what would be a lifelong love affair with the city.

By his second year in Quebec, Beliveau was again too good for the company he kept. He scored 61 goals and added

63 assists. By now, Beliveau had met his first and only girl-friend, Elise Coutu, a lovely, bilingual Québécoise who knew nothing of hockey.

After Beliveau's second and final year of junior eligibility, the Citadels presented him with a 1951 Nash Rambler as a token of appreciation and Beliveau's loyalty to the city deepened even further. When the independant Quebec Aces began play in the Quebec Senior league, Beliveau was told he would be paid whatever Montreal might offer to stay in Quebec City. He stayed two years, earning $10,000 in his first season and $20,000 in his second. That salary was believed to be the equivalent of what Maurice Richard was making in Montreal and the gifted giant in Quebec City became a fixation across the hockey world. Frank Mahovlich, playing junior with Toronto's St. Mikes, heard a rumor along the players' grapevine that Beliveau owned 15 suits.

"I did have a lot of suits, it's true," laughs Beliveau. "There was a store in Quebec that would give me a suit and socks every time I made a hat trick. As a matter of fact, I had so many socks I ended up dividing them between my team-mates."

Finally, after four years in Quebec City, Beliveau sensed it was time to move on. "I would be turning 22 in August after my second year with the Quebec Aces and four years in Quebec City, and I said it's about time we moved to Montreal. I wanted to play for the Canadiens. At that time, a good career was 15 years. Boy, if I wanted that 15 years, I'd have to keep playing until I was 37."

Playing in Quebec City not only netted Beliveau the equivalent of a top NHL salary, it also gave him a very strong negotiating stance with the Canadiens. That position was enhanced dramatically when in stints in 1951 and 1952 with the Canadiens, Beliveau was dominant, scoring six goals in five games.

Jean and Elise married in the summer of 1952 and at the 1953 all-star break, the Canadiens finally capitulated to Beliveau's demands with an unheard of starting salary of $25,000. But after the hype that surrounded his signing, his total of 13 goals and 34 points over 44 games in 1953 seemed a disappointment. His second year, a 37-goal, 73-point effort, showcased his brilliant skills, but a problem was emerging. Beliveau, a solid but gentlemanly competitor, was sometimes nullified by cheap shots and late hits. His production had been impeded by a series of injuries and he was beginning to get a reputation that he could be intimidated.

"Hitting people wasn't his nature and it isn't his way of life today," said his old linemate Bert Olmstead. "But, I think he realized it was time to stand up and be counted. Plus, by his third season, he had gotten the stuff he could get away with in amateur and senior hockey out of his system."

In 1955–56, Beliveau decided to do with size what he had always done with skill: dominate. He didn't roam the ice looking for people to hit, he just made sure he would be making the dent in any collision. Beliveau's penalty minutes soared from 58 to a career high and club record 143, and as his aggressiveness peaked, so did the other elements of his game. "Everything, his shooting, his passing, his skating," Olmstead recalled. "Everything was better."

Beliveau scored 47 goals and logged 88 points in 70 games as he won both the Hart Trophy as the league's most valuable player and outdistanced Gordie Howe by nine points for the scoring championship. Beliveau kept it up in the playoffs, scoring seven times in the Canadiens' five-game Cup victory over Detroit and collecting at least one goal in each game. Beliveau's 12 post-season goals tied Richard's league record.

Beliveau was 24 years old and in his absolute prime. "I think he had a gift," said Mahovlich. "His size and the way he moved was a natural gift. Everything just flowed from that and he had a lot of grace to go with it."

"He was one of a kind, a classic," said New York Rangers Hall-of-Famer Rod Gilbert. "Jean Beliveau was probably the best player ever in the NHL. He was a typical centerman with lanky strides and vision to both sides. You talk about Wayne Gretzky, Mario Lemieux, Beliveau was as good as them during our time."

Beliveau's brilliance, preserved for the modern day on videotape, bears a striking resemblance to the genius Mario Lemieux displays 30 years later. It is most evident in their stride and their reach. Beliveau held the puck closer to his body and protected it better than Lemieux does, and Lemieux, at least before back troubles curtailed his stride, was probably a faster skater. But both players were the dominant stickhandlers of their eras and their focus seemed to sharpen as they drew closer to the net.

"I think Lemieux has the greatest hands I've seen on any big man but Beliveau's hands were awful close," said Rangers Hall-of-Famer Harry Howell, now a scout with the Edmonton Oilers. "Beliveau is a big man so he was awful hard to move in front of the net. All you could really do was try to get his stick off the ice."

Still, the demands on Beliveau were unending. Two-goal games only brought cries for a hat trick, winning only deepened the demand for more victory. Crank calls, media inquisitons and suffocating pressure were part of his daily life.

Winning made the process worthwhile. The 1955 Cup victory was the first in what would be a run of five straight championships for the Canadiens. Beliveau apprenticed with the best, as Butch Bouchard and Rocket Richard wore the C during those championship years. When Maurice Richard retired in 1960, Doug Harvey donned the C but Harvey lasted only a season before being dispatched to the New York Rangers. In the fall of 1961, Beliveau joined the club for the traditional secret vote for the captain at the final practice prior to the beginning of the season. He had injured his knee in an exhibition game and would be out until Christmas. He hadn't even been an assistant captain prior to the vote. "I almost fell off the bench in the room when Toe came back, shook my hand and said 'Boys, here's your new captain.'"

The vote had been close, even divisive. The captaincy had been coveted by Boom Boom Geoffrion, Beliveau's rightwinger and roommate, who bolted from the Forum as soon as the announcement was made. Because of Geoffrion's hurt feelings, Beliveau, who considered it automatic that a player with more service like Geoffrion, Tom Johnson or Dickie Moore would get the C, initially took little joy in the players' decision.

Making the move even more problematic was the fact that Rocket Richard, retired but still and always an icon in Montreal, thought Geoffrion, a more engaging and charismatic personality and a man coming off the only other 50-goal season in franchise history, was the proper choice. "The players voted and Beliveau won but personally, I think the management pressured the players to pick Beliveau," Richard would later write. "I think it was a great mistake. For one thing, Geoffrion had seniority on the team; and that was something that should have been respected. For another, I think being bypassed like that was the worst thing that could have happened to the sensitive Boomer. After he was rejected by his teammates, the Boomer was never the same guy for Les Canadiens. It changed him completely. Had he been named captain I think the Canadiens would have been just as good as they were with Beliveau, if not better, and the players would have had more fun with him than with Beliveau."

After a week of soul searching, Beliveau decided to give the letter back. "I never expected it and I've always thought I was a team player," Beliveau tearfully told Canadiens' general manager Frank Selke. "The most important thing is the good of the team." Selke refused Beliveau's request. "I can't go in the room and tell the players we're going to put in Geoffrion and not you," Selke said. "If Geoffrion isn't happy, that's his problem."

Geoffrion did in fact slip to seasons of 23, 23 and 21 goals before being traded to the New York Rangers but that decline was caused by persistent health problems. And there was no disputing the players' choice, based on the success Beliveau and the Canadiens would go on to enjoy during his captaincy. Montreal was back in the Cup finals in 1965 and Beliveau captured the first-ever Conn Smythe Trophy for playoff MVP in the club's seven-game defeat of Chicago. In 13 playoff games, Beliveau scored eight times and got as many assists. A year later, he scored three times in the final as the Canadiens defeated Detroit in six games. The Canadiens returned to the finals in 1967 but this time Toronto outlasted Montreal in six games. Beliveau, with four goals, tied for the finals lead in goals with Henri Richard and Toronto's Jim Pappin.

Injuries kept Beliveau out of all but one game of the 1968 finals but again the Canadiens prevailed, this time over St. Louis. Beliveau and Montreal returned the following year and again overcame the Blues in four games.

Through the 1960s, Beliveau and the Canadiens had appeared in six finals, winning five, and Beliveau's 12 goals in the Stanley Cup finals were more than any player's total in the decade. Almost as importantly, Beliveau evolved from the reluctant to the quintessential captain, again melding formidable natural gifts with a relentless sense of industry.

"In Montreal, there were really three roles for Canadiens' captains," Beliveau recalled. "First, you're the person between the coach and the players. You have to listen to your teammates and try to solve every [minor] problem, which, often to a young rookie, seems to be a major one. It could be a youngster having a personal problem or a difficult situation. You have to manage to make them feel better without them feeling you're putting your nose in their personal business. From the start, I said I'm available on anything at any time.

"Secondly, you have to be the person who goes between the players and the coach and the referee. The third thing in Montreal was representing the team. At that time, there was a lot of representation involved on nights when you were not playing. Now, since they play every second night, the captain doesn't have to worry that much about it."

It was a role for which Beliveau was marvelously cast. The evidence can be found on the inscriptions on the Stanley Cup; it can also be found in the reminiscences of former teammates. "When I first came up to the Montreal Canadiens, I stayed a week at Jean's place," remembered Guy Lafleur. "He was helping me out with the pressure I was having at that time. It was really nice and very important to me because he had always been my idol."

When Dick Duff was traded to the Canadiens, he sought out Beliveau and asked him if there was anything special he wanted him to do on the ice. Beliveau smiled broadly and said two words: "Just play." After the fifth game of the 1971 final against Chicago, Henri Richard, furious at being benched, labeled his coach, Al MacNeil, an incompetent in a post-game tirade recorded by Bertrand Raymond of *Le Journal de Montréal*. Beliveau walked by, exchanged a look with Richard and squeezed his arm. "After that," Raymond has said, "I couldn't get any kind of quote out of Henri."

There would be one final Stanley Cup for a Beliveau-led team. Beliveau scored six goals and added a record 16 assists in the 1971 Stanley Cup victory. He was 39 years old when he left hockey as the all-time leader in playoff assists (97) and points (176). The victory was his tenth Stanley Cup. Henri Richard, with 11, was the only player who won more. Beliveau retired with 507 regular season goals, then second only to Rocket Richard in the club's history. In post-season play he scored another 79 goals, three fewer than Richard. Beliveau was ready for the Canadiens at 18 and had he joined the NHL at that time, he, not Richard, would have held the record as the club's most prolific goalscoring forward.

When he announced his retirement on June 9, 1971, at the Queen Elizabeth Hotel, Beliveau was accorded the rarest of tributes. Even the media gave him a standing ovation.

There would be one final temptation to play. When the World Hockey Association's Quebec Nordiques began play in 1972, then-general manager Jacques Plante offered Beliveau $1 million over four years to return to Quebec City for a curtain call. To qualify for the $1 million, Beliveau only had to play one season, he would earn the rest as an executive over the balance of his contract. "I met with them, but I told them, whatever you offer me, it wouldn't be honest for you, for your team, for the fans or for myself," Beliveau recalled. "I said 'I will be over 40 and I know I cannot play the type of game I should be playing for you.' I respected that the money you offered was more than I earned during these 18 years with the Canadiens, but I felt that I couldn't play the type of game I enjoyed. That would not have been honest."

Beliveau had worked for the Molson's publicity department throughout his career with the Canadiens and expected to move from the team directly into the brewery, where he had already accrued 18 years of seniority. Instead, David Molson and Canadiens' general manager Sam Pollock persuaded Beliveau to remain with the hockey club in a series of jobs that ended with his being named vice-president of corporate relations.

He would prove himself a hands-on executive. Beliveau argued against the hiring of then-coach Scotty Bowman as general manager in 1978. He had seen Bowman try to talk Sam Pollock into trading players after one or two bad games and was sure Bowman's impatience would devastate the organization. Unfortunately for Montreal, when Bowman left for Buffalo, the club chose Irving Grundman, the worst general manager in its history. It was Beliveau who oversaw the care of many Canadiens alumni. When Toe Blake's Alzheimer's Disease made institutionalizing him necessary, Beliveau gathered the family to determine the best course of action.

Politics has tugged at Beliveau throughout his post-playing career. Twice, most recently in 1992, he turned down then-Prime Minister Brian Mulroney's attempts to press him into service as a senator. "I never wanted to be involved in politics," Beliveau said. "I had been asked as a player to maybe go as an MP, but I said no. I wanted to help society in my own way with different children's organizations mostly. Plus, I always felt the Senate should be elected."

In October of 1989, Beliveau looked up from his desk at the Forum to see two Montreal police officers. His son-in-law Serge, a 25-year-veteran of the Montreal Urban Community Police Department, had shot himself while despondent over marital troubles. In addition to widowing Beliveau's only child Hélène, the suicide left her two daughters, Mylene and Magalie, without a father. It fell to Beliveau to inform Hélène and the children of the death of his son-in-law and the suicide induced him to turn down the most prestigious offer he had ever received. Prime Minister Jean Chrétien began sounding Beliveau out in 1994 over his willingness to become the new governor general and an offer was soon on the table. "My only child is a widow with daughters eight and ten," Beliveau said. "I strongly feel it's my duty to be the father those girls need for the next five years or so. Therefore, what I told Mr. Chrétien was that to take my wife and move to Ottawa would be deserting my family."

Grandchildren and grandparents live five minutes apart by car and they see each other frequently. On most game nights, Hélène and one of the girls are at the Molson Centre using Beliveau's seats. Grandma and Grandpa watch the game on television, often from the girls' house.

"You don't replace a father but sometimes we travel with them," Beliveau said. "Many times we take them out, they enjoy going to the Forum. You bring them to the Imax Theatre, you bring them to different places. We never miss a chance to be with them and though we don't see them every day, they know we are here. All they have to do is grab the phone and we'll be there."

Beliveau finally left the Canadiens on his 62nd birthday, August 31, 1993, but still makes goodwill appearances on behalf of the team and Molson's. He cut the number of boards he sits on to four and finds renewal in a scaled-down schedule that allows more time for his wife, daughter and grandchildren.

The dark brown hair has long since passed into a striking silver and his charges are two little girls, rather than the world's best hockey team, but things have not changed that much for Jean Beliveau. He leads even now and when asked whether doting on two adoring grandchildren compares with winning the Stanley Cup, he gently asks for an indulgence. "I'm very proud of them and my daughter and the Stanley Cup, well that is always a great joy because you accomplish what you started at the beginning of the year," said Beliveau. "Allow me, please, to be very proud of both."

CHAPTER 6

HENRI RICHARD

CAPTAIN 1971–1975

CHAPTER 6

HENRI RICHARD

CAPTAIN 1971–1975

The men and women on the bus were having a good time. After a sumptuous buffet, Montreal Canadiens of various eras and contributions, among them Don Awrey, Tom Johnson, Dick Duff, Gump Worsley and their wives, were about to be shuttled from the Queen Elizabeth Hotel to the last Montreal Canadiens game at the Forum.

Somewhere in the hotel Henri Richard had been detained and the veterans were growing good-naturedly impatient. "To hell with it, let's go without him," joked an anonymous player from the back of the bus. "Hey, now" came a reproachful voice from the same area. "That's the Rocket's brother we're talking about."

To the Montreal Canadiens as well as their followers, Henri Richard will always be the Rocket's brother, the "Pocket Rocket." It can be written now that no amount of success or leadership, no run of championships can blur that link because no professional hockey player has enjoyed more of these gifts than Henri Richard yet, as the boys in the back of the bus will attest, he remains first and foremost the Rocket's little brother.

All this troubles Henri Richard not a bit. He is a wealthy man, both from his NHL career and from the profits of the hugely successful tavern that he ran for 26 years. He keeps a summer home in Florida, the better to indulge his passion for tennis. Two weeks after surgery to insert a balloon-type instrument and clear some minor obstructions in his arteries, he is tanned and fit. The shock of white hair, trimmed neatly, is nonetheless striking. But for the bifocals he wears while sorting through the morning mail in his office at a Laval, Quebec, industrial park, he looks no older than he did on the day in 1975 he retired as a Montreal Canadien.

Fate handed Henri Richard good and bad fortune in largely equal measures. Accorded a bantamweight boxer's body (Richard played at 5'7" and 165 pounds) he was allotted a heavyweight's heart. Although he grew up in poverty, he was given, through hockey, the means to make good. The brother of an icon, Henri Richard had the strength of character it took never to try to compete with him.

He was and is the rarest of commodities, the truly self-made man who focused his gifts so superbly that his limitations became advantages. Not having to drag 200 pounds around the ice meant he could skate longer and to greater effect. "You can take Beliveau and all the others," said former Canadiens' general manager Ken Reardon. "Give me Henri. That little bugger could skate for five minutes without getting tired."

Since he was usually the smallest player on the ice, he was also the most nimble. As Maurice Richard's brother, he received less attention from opposing checkers and hometown media than that accorded to his charismatic brother, and he flourished in the extra space.

If a comparison must be made, consider that Henri Richard was a better all-around player than his brother. Maurice Richard focused every movement of his game on scoring and with 544 regular season goals, collected 186 more than Henri.

The younger Richard played more seasons (20–18), games (1,256–978), and accrued more regular season points (1,046–965), playoff points (129–126) and Stanley Cups (11–8). Like Dave Keon, Richard took most of his turns against the opposition's top lines and he was an inexhaustible defensive player who averaged 18 goals a year. A prodigious goalscorer in Junior, he graduated to the NHL as a set-up artist for his brother's final five years in the league, and Henri was a premier penalty-killer from the moment he stepped into the NHL.

A more fitting comparison establishes Richard's record in the context of all four major sports. Henri Richard and Boston Celtics star Bill Russell are the most prodigious winners big league sports ever produced, sharing the standard for most championships won: 11. Yogi Berra of the New York Yankees won ten, while a handful of NFL players, including Green Bay Packers' quarterback Bart Starr, have won five championships. Conversations about Henri Richard invariably begin with a mention of his brother and end with a shake of the head over the volume of his Stanley Cup successes.

"I admit it," Richard says, smiling at the retelling. "I was lucky. Had I been in any other city, New York or Chicago,

I wouldn't have won nearly as many. Dick Duff likes to tease me about that, he says I'm lucky. I say 'Dickie, I agree with you.'"

But no one worked harder for good luck. Richard did not rise above his stature to become a star; his size shaped and defined him. "What made Henri Richard a great player was desire," said longtime friend and teammate Jean-Guy Talbot. "When you were small, you had to have more desire than anybody else to survive."

"The guy was a complete competitor," said former Canadien Peter Mahovlich. "They say there's no room for small players in the game. I'll tell you something, if they have the same fire and drive that Henri Richard had, there's always room for players like that."

Richard's father was 45 when he was born and by the time young Henri was six, his brother Maurice was married and had moved out of the house. The eight Richard children grew up poor in a small home in Bordeaux, a working-class area of Montreal.

"We had no money," recalled Richard. "My father would work repairing freight trains and he didn't make much. My sister was closer in age to us and my younger brother and I would wear some of her clothes. My mother used to buy a ham on Saturday and have it for the whole week, through Thursday. There was no meat on Friday. We had to wash in a tub, there was no bathroom. Like most poor kids, we didn't know anything different."

Richard cannot recall life without the questions: Was he another Rocket? Would he grow big enough to play in the NHL? By the time he reached his teens, his natural ability was beyond dispute, but at 16, he weighed 90 pounds and the more he played, the less he seemed to grow. "People didn't think hockey was in my future but everywhere I went, they said 'There's Maurice's brother,' " Richard said. "I had to have something to tell them, so when they asked, I told them I wanted to be a bricklayer. That's what my sister's boyfriend did, he was a bricklayer. But really, playing hockey like my brother was the only thing I had in my mind."

Instead of center, where he would incur less contact, coaches assigned the 120-pound Richard the right wing, the same side as his brother. "My first coach in Junior was Elmer Lach and I don't hold it against him but he told me I was too small," Richard remembers now. He allows himself a wry smile. "But 20 years in the NHL, that's not too bad."

In fact, by the time he was 19, Richard was simply too skilled to ignore. Richard attended his first Canadiens' camp as a 16-year-old and after three years it became a rite of fall that he would hold his own and, in some cases, even outplay NHL veterans. "We had to sign him," Toe Blake once said. "At camp, he took the puck and nobody could take it away from him. He was just too good not to sign."

Canadiens general manager Frank Selke, as well as assistant general manager Ken Reardon, initially thought Richard should be sent to the minors to acclimatize himself to the rugged game he would encounter in the NHL. Maurice interceded and pointed out that the abuse Henri would receive in the more loosely officiated levels of minor pro was probably worse than any he would encounter in the big leagues. Reardon and Selke agreed, and in the fall of 1955, the Richard brothers were called into the club's office.

The younger Richard spoke no English so Selke addressed his question to Maurice. "Is your brother ready to sign?" he asked. Maurice Richard said yes, stood up and left the room. This was an affair between his brother and his boss.

Selke proffered a scrap of paper torn out of a daytimer and jotted down the terms of the two-year contract: signing bonus $5,000, $8,000 a year should Richard stick with the Canadiens. If Maurice negotiated his brother's salary, he kept it to himself and the signing of that first contract was perfectly in keeping with the relationship between the brothers. Because of the age gap and the lack of common experiences that chasm created, the brothers are not close. Maurice Richard, for example, hasn't been to his brother's house in decades. This does not mean that they are not proud of each other, they are fiercely so, but the Richards, like most siblings from different generations, really shared little more than common bloodlines and backgrounds.

"Maurice was immensely proud of 'my kid brother' but in a reserved way," *Weekend Magazine* writer Andy O'Brien once noted. "Even on road trips, they'd never sit together and just chat. Maurice would be playing cards while Henri was over in a corner of the car, plugging away at an English magazine, pausing now and then to consult an ever-present French-English dictionary."

Throughout his career, Henri Richard maintained a younger brother's deference toward his older sibling. Where Richard's teammates called him Rocket or Rock, Henri called him Maurice and their relationship was more like that of a father and son than two brothers. Once Maurice and Henri collided and knocked each other cold playing on the same line in an exhibition contest. When the Rocket woke up, he said to a still-groggy Henri: "You'd better take care of yourself Henri, you're liable to get yourself hurt."

The two never talked about hockey and did not inhabit the same inner circles inside the Canadiens. "That team had a lot of leaders, Rocket, Bert Olmstead," said Winnipeg Jets' scout Connie Broden, who came up at about the same time as Richard. "When the two groups were together, the young guys shut up. It was the old guys who ran the show."

Henri Richard is neither boastful nor envious of the fervor Rocket Richard still prompts from Quebec's hockey fans. He considers his brother his greatest influence but has no answer when asked what made him such an enduring icon.

Richard was dubbed "the Pocket Rocket" while still in Junior. The Canadiens were scheduled to play in Toronto one Saturday night and the Marlboros would host the Junior Canadiens Sunday afternoon. An enterprising copywriter for a Toronto newspaper devised an ad: "Come and see the Rocket play on Saturday night and the Pocket Rocket play on Sunday." Henri Richard was the Pocket Rocket forever more.

"I didn't mind [the nickname]," Richard recalls, "but a lot of people wanted me to write it as my signature. I never would. It doesn't bother me, not at all. It happens still, the fathers and [their] sons [who] might be 12 years old . . . point at me, they say look, there's Maurice Richard's brother."

When he arrived in the NHL, Richard won immediate respect for the way he handled the inevitable comparisons. "Other players taunted him, they called him Maurice but it never seemed to bother him," said Olmstead. "He was one of my favorite players. When you had a brother like Rocket, you were kind of handicapped but it never seemed to bother him."

Far more problematic for Richard was mastering English. Canadiens teammates Dickie Moore and Doug Harvey were the first English speakers he spent any measure of time with and his status as a rookie, combined with the language barrier, made his first years in the NHL terribly lonely. Prior to Richard's first game, he got lost between the hotel and the Boston Garden and couldn't ask passersby for help.

Until he mastered English, Richard remained quiet. He would say "me too" in a restaurant when a teammate ordered, usually without knowing what he was getting. He was so awestruck by the Forum, he did not feel comfortable enough to shave there for ten years. Toe Blake was once asked if his young center could speak English. "I don't even know if he can speak French," Blake replied.

Richard began the season on the right side when Boom Boom Geoffrion suffered an early-season shoulder injury. "They put me with Beliveau and Olmstead," recalls Richard. "That was my very first shift and I was nervous like hell. Bert he would give me shit if I didn't do like he told me. I felt like I had my head between my legs the whole time."

Even with his fiery brother nearby, he was tested often. He quickly proved himself eager to return whatever attempts at intimidation he encountered. "There's quite a few that tried," recalled Richard. "I never backed off, I used to jump in their face. That was my style. Sometimes, you would pretend quite a bit you weren't scared, sometimes you were."

For a small man, Richard was a punishing fighter. Former Red Wing Marty Pavelich once regaled a newspaperman about a New Year's Day, 1958, fight he saw Richard wage in Boston. "First thing, Henri hauled off and hit (Leo) Labine, and split his eyebrow for a dozen stitches. That put Labine out. Then Jack Bionda came in and Bionda was big. Richard hit him and split his nose. Twisted it across his face. That put Bionda out. Now it was up to (Fernie) Flaman. Flaman really was one of the toughest guys in the league and he didn't lose too many. But he didn't beat Henri. It was about a draw. I never would have believed it if I hadn't seen it with my own eyes."

Richard scored 19 times in his rookie season (1956–57) and quickly erased any doubt about his ability to be an NHLer. Hawks coach Rudy Pilous watched Richard dominate one game and spoke for the whole league. "Looks like Henri Richard brought his own puck to the rink again," he said.

Richard's arrival coincided with the Canadiens' remarkable run of five consecutive Stanley Cups and Richard scored seven goals and added 15 assists in 25 Stanley Cup final games. After a four-year dry spell, the Canadiens regained the Cup in 1965 in a seven-game victory over Chicago, and Richard netted the Cup winner in 1966 as the Canadiens out-lasted Detroit.

The goal remains controversial. Game Six in Detroit was in overtime when Toe Blake tapped Richard on the shoulder. "Go on in Henri," Blake said, "You're going to get the winner." Moments later, Richard drove the net. He was tripped and the puck lodged in his equipment as he skidded past Detroit netminder Roger Crozier. Blake immediately sent his team over the boards and referee Frank Udvari let the goal stand.

"I don't know myself how the puck went in," recalled Richard. "I always remember Crozier saying I pushed it in with my hand. I never said a bloody thing. When you watched the replay, you couldn't say where it went in, from the shoulder or where. But then again, if Crozier had played it the way most of the goalies played it and tried to protect the guy going in against the post, the puck would never have gone in."

In his thirties, Richard's game was in full flower. He was fearless going into the corner for the puck and defended the territory he had staked out ferociously. "I remember the only time Henri and I had words," said John Ferguson. "We were in New York, and he got in a fight with Jim Neilson [a 6'2" defenseman] and I stepped in and took over. We got in an argument later because Henri was really peeved at me. He thought it looked like he couldn't fight his own battles."

By then, Richard had developed a full repertoire of tricks to gain favor with officials. "One of the things he used to do when he went wide on me was lean into me and actually grab my knee," recalled former Bruins defenseman Fernie Flaman. "We'd both go down and I would get the penalty for holding because it was impossible to see what Henri was doing. It used to drive me crazy."

Beliveau captained the Canadiens for 14 of Richard's seasons and the two operated as a superb tandem. Beliveau, diplomatic and regal, personified elegance. Richard, chippy and fearless, represented grit. "Henri was definitely a leader, even before he was captain," Beliveau said. "His leadership came from his determination on the ice and the fact that he was a team player."

"I'll tell you how Henri led," Ferguson said. "He was the same guy in every building we went into, Boston, New York, Chicago. It didn't matter a bit to him."

Richard garnered Cup number seven in 1968 and three years later scored the tying and winning goals as the Canadiens, behind rookie goalie Ken Dryden, defeated the Hawks in seven games. Richard was now 35 and aside from Beliveau, stood as the club's elder statesman. But when rookie coach Al MacNeil benched Richard for two periods in Game Five, which was a loss to Chicago, Richard sounded off to the Francophone media, labeling MacNeil an "incompetent" and the worst coach he had ever played for.

MacNeil, an Anglophone, was instantly cast as the villain and while Richard ultimately acquitted himself superbly with his Game Seven performance, he has always regretted the political dimensions the story quickly assumed. "Whatever I said, I didn't really mean it." Richard said. "Al MacNeil is a hell of a guy, too nice to be a coach. Then it turned out to be something with the language and all that shit. It had nothing to do with language, I was not playing, I was mad, and that was it."

MacNeil received death threats over the incident and was accompanied by security guards in the Forum. He was gone the next year and with the retirement of Beliveau, Richard was voted captain.

Teammates remember him as an exemplary captain who wasn't afraid to oppose management. Even as Richard's talents began to ebb with age, the shadow of his Stanley Cups lent greater authority to his standing. "The short answer I've always given about Maurice Richard's ability to lead was 'Look at his eyes,'" Beliveau said. "With Henri, you could say, 'Look what he's done.'"

"Henri Richard helped me a lot when I first came up with the team," remembered Guy Lafleur. "I was not playing much, and he and Yvan talked to me a lot and said don't get discouraged, play my game instead of the way Scotty Bowman wanted me to play. They told me just be myself and play the way I did in Junior."

"Henri had 19 years in the league and 11 Stanley Cups," recalled former Canadien Doug Risebrough. " I was so thankful that a man who had done everything in hockey, still was willing to offer to a 20-year-old player like myself, encouragement. He was willing to be one of the boys. I remember at one of the Christmas parties, Henri's daughter was older than I was. But what really made Henri a great captain is when he walked out the dressing room door, you knew you were going to get 100 percent."

Henri Richard spent very little effort on being a captain. He devoted his energy to being himself. "A leader is a pretty big word," Richard said. "I never took being named captain as that big a thing. You've got to have one. Today there is much more responsibility." "Henri never talked too much," said former Canadien Yvon Lambert. "He was working so hard, in practice, in games, he didn't have time to talk."

Even as he battled Bowman over the club's style and playing time, Richard insisted on doing the right thing. In 1972, angry that Bowman had sat him out in Vancouver, he slapped Serge Savard in a dressing room fight. Savard was one of several players angry about a recent story who wanted to lock the media out of the dressing room. "I came into the room. The trainer used to ask the coach if we would let the newspaper in. Savard said, "Screw those guys.' I said, 'Why don't you shut your mouth. Don't say something like that. They're the people who pay your salary actually.' So he said, 'You go and sleep with those guys.' I got up [to take] a swing at him, and I changed my mind and just slapped him. That was it."

Richard later berated Bowman during a practice for a remark he made about Savard's divorce. "I said 'Screw off Bowman.' I never liked him as a coach. He knows hockey but I didn't like his attitude, the way he attempted to prove things to you. But he's a hell of a coach."

Richard presided over one more Stanley Cup victory in 1973 as the club decisioned the Black Hawks in six games. He enjoyed a 19-goal campaign at 38 but after scoring just three goals in 1974–75, Henri Richard retired at the age of 40. He had $125,000 left on his contract but felt he was no longer able to earn it.

It has been a busy retirement. Richard sold his pub in 1985 after a 26-year-run and keeps a steady stream of public relations appointments for Molson's Brewery. Restless at home, he opened his office to give him something else to do during the day, but like every Quebecker, he keeps a close eye on the province's volatile political situation.

The image of Maurice Richard, still so potent in Quebec, was long ago conscripted by nationalists as a symbol of dogged self-determination. His brother, the winningest hockey player in NHL history, remains a federalist.

"You're damn right I'm not a separatist," Richard said. "I always remember my wife would call Eaton's; they'd say I'm sorry we don't speak French. Or people wouldn't serve you, they wouldn't speak French. But I'm a Canadian. I just love Canadians, whatever the language or color. This [the nationalist movement] is something that I really feel is too bad."

No state can exist without ideology and the man behind the desk is one of the most heralded contributors to the institution many think has supplanted the Church as the dominant spiritual institution in Quebec: the Montreal Canadiens. That means that in the eyes of Quebeckers, Henri Richard is at the very least a Cardinal. "Yes," says Henri Richard, smiling broadly at the idea. "I suppose that is true."

It's a good thought to leave with at the conversation's end. As he returns to the papers on his desk, Henri Richard takes for granted the identity of the Pope.

CHAPTER 7

YVAN COURNOYER

CAPTAIN 1975–1979

YVAN COURNOYER

CAPTAIN 1975–1979

He is 53 now, but the man sitting in the stands in the Montreal Forum looks very much like the one who toiled so successfully a few feet away on the business side of the dasher boards. Everything about his face, the cherub features, impossibly high cheekbones and merry eyes, have been left intact by time.

Unlike many powerful smaller men, Yvan Cournoyer did not become more barrel-chested as he aged; in fact, his present silhouette would be almost identical to his outline as a player.

It has been nearly 20 years since his retirement, but Cournoyer still speaks of his final days as a player with a disarming wistfulness reserved for a love long lost. "You know," Cournoyer said in soft, even tones, "it took me five years to really, really, realize it was over. I had signed a contract for three more years and I scored two goals against Philadelphia and I said to my son, 'I think your father's back.' The next day, I couldn't get out of bed."

At 35, age, in lockstep with injury, accomplished what scores of defensemen could not, ground the least earthbound of the Montreal Canadiens. "I've always said, the best day of my life was when I made the Montreal Canadiens," Cournoyer said ruefully. "The worst day of my life was when I retired."

Eighteen years later he is back home, as a coach and, for one final time, a player. Tomorrow he will skate with an alumni team of Montreal Canadiens in an old-timers' game at the Forum. The night after, March 11, the current Canadiens will play there for the last time.

"This is my last game, ever," said Cournoyer, "and I think this is my way of closing the building. I remember I was 17 years old when I first came here, I was playing for the Junior Canadiens. This is like moving from the house where you grew up and to say goodbye to this one, where there are so many memories, it'll be quite something."

Cournoyer should not play; his back and knees, the subject of intrusive surgeries while he played, are now more or less normal. He grudgingly retired in 1978 when doctors warned him another comeback would risk permanent spinal damage, but like a spirit that goes too soon, he has never really been free of the place. Pride provokes an urge to play, but it also exerts another pull, even greater: the desire to quit, to leave the memory of his game untarnished by not taking too many curtain calls.

"I'm recognized to be fast on the ice," Cournoyer said. "When you don't have the chance to play or to practice, the people are disappointed. The father says to the son, watch number 12, but he's disappointed because you're not fast anymore. I don't want that."

One of Cournoyer's skating secrets lay in the hollow of his blade; he insisted his skates have the longest possible blade to increase the speed that comes when steel meets ice. Powerful legs, a precise and energetic stride and perfectly doctored skates gave Cournoyer his premium speed but Cournoyer could neither turn nor stop as well most of the other players on the ice. "The turnaround," Cournoyer said with a grin, "did not compensate for the lost speed."

Cournoyer built his game on Richardian elements, superb speed and a fearlessness in going to the net. The Soviets called the 5'7", 178-pound right winger "The Train". Everyone else used "Roadrunner", a name coined by a *Sports Illustrated* reporter who had seen Cournoyer score two electrifying goals at Madison Square Garden.

"His shot, his skating, everything about him is full speed," goaltending great Gump Worsley once said. "How do you stop anybody like that?"

Through the 1960s and much of the 1970s, Yvan Cournoyer was the fastest man in the National Hockey League. Speed, not power, is the most redoubtable gift a hockey player can possess. It can be used on offense and defense, late in the game or early and it constantly heightens the sense of risk felt by defensemen. Speed *is* possibility and the players who possess it are revered by their peers.

"I saw him for he first time in 1972," remembered Soviet goaltending great Vladislav Tretiak. "I looked up and I thought, oh, that's a very fast guy. Very fast and smart. The last game we played Team Canada in Canada, 1972 in Vancouver, maybe 20 seconds apart, he had two breakaways on me. He was an unbelievable player."

Cournoyer won 10 Stanley Cups including four consecutive between 1976 and 1979 and along with Howie Morenz,

Dave Keon and Henri Richard, he stood among the best small men to ever play.

Despite all this, Cournoyer is best remembered not for what he did but for how he played with his trademark speed and a sheer, unmistakable joy. "I never met a man who enjoyed playing more than Yvan," said former teammate Doug Risebrough. "He had that great big smile and he smiled as much scoring goals in practice as he did during games."

No one loved to score more than Maurice Richard, no one loved to play more than Yvan Cournoyer. Winning was always a marvelous and powerful incentive but playing—nothing could top playing. Winning just made playing even better.

"Hockey, it's a challenge, every game is different," Cournoyer said. "You lose, you ask yourself, what am I going to do now to win. You win one, you say what am I going to do keep on winning. Your mind is always working. The day of the game, your hands are wet, the adrenaline comes up and after he game, you go down as you relax. You cannot find that in anything but sport, especially here in Montreal."

Yvan Cournoyer, like Jean Beliveau, was the product of small town Quebec, he grew up in Drummondville, an hour Northeast of Montreal. His father Paul worked as a machinist in Montreal and commuted every weekend back to Drummondville. Simone Cournoyer looked after five children, with Yvan the second eldest. "We were not rich," Cournoyer said, "but when television came out we had a TV and when a fridge came out we had a fridge. My father always had a nice car."

Cournoyer began playing hockey at seven when his uncle bought him his first pair of skates as a birthday present. Paul Cournoyer kept a rink beside the house and his son toiled relentlessly at the game, he took a job at the local arena to garner more ice time and raced to be the first to shovel outdoor rinks to strengthen his leg drive. His father made him a weighted puck, which he used throughout the summer to improve his shot.

"It was always my dream," Cournoyer said, flatly, "to play for the Montreal Canadiens."

Paul bought a machine shop in Montreal and moved his family to the city when Yvan was 13. Cournoyer quickly worked his way up through the minor hockey system but still found time to earn his machinist papers at 15. Had hockey not panned out, he planned to follow his father into the trade but that would be the only concession young Yvan would make to the idea that his future might not include the NHL.

Cournoyer once scored 63 for the Montreal Junior Canadiens and finally skated for Montreal in 1963–64, when he scored four goals in five games.

The next season, Cournoyer scored seven times but despite steady pressure from the Francophone media, coach Toe Blake used Cournoyer all but exclusively on the power play. In the 1968–69 playoffs, Cournoyer was benched in a tight-checking semi final against Boston in favor of Claude Provost. By now, he had broken the 20-goal plateau and the benching wounded his pride, prompting Cournoyer to redouble his efforts on defensive play.

"I think it's as important to do as good defensively as offensively," Cournoyer said. "One year, I finished plus-20 and that was a great achievement. You'll play more at the end of the game and at the end of the period of you have a commitment to the team."

Cournoyer would emerge as a four-time all-star and a Conn Smythe winner in 1972–73 when he led the playoffs with 15 goals and 25 points in 17 games. Twice he led the Canadiens in scoring and he once collected a five goal game.

Cournoyer was 30 when he was selected to play for Canada in the 1972 Summit Series. He scored three goals as Canada outlasted the Soviets in eight games and the sequence that led to Paul Henderson's series-winning goal began with Cournoyer playing a hunch. It was a typical Cournoyer play, built on equal parts speed and extra effort.

"In Russia, it was near the end of the game and my left wing went out, my centreman went out, and I just wanted to come out," Cournoyer remembered. "The puck went into their zone, 'I said shit, one more time.' Like I said, I had decided to go out and they didn't see me go back. That's where I intercepted the pass. Paul Henderson came from the bench and Phil Esposito came from the bench. I tried to reach Paul but somebody tripped him. The puck went around and Phil picked up the puck. By that time, Paul got up and got in front and bingo."

Henderson's goal, as much as any Stanley Cup win, was one of the telling moments of Cournoyer's career. That historic moment, Cournoyer has told countless corporate executives, was built on the joy that comes with doing something you love.

"If I go to the bench, there is no goal. That's why if you like your job and do something you like to do and if you're willing to give some extra, you're going to be better than somebody else. I used that a lot for talks with corporations. If someone looks at his watch and it's 5 o'clock and he wants to go home and he's pissed off every time he works a little over-time, he should do something else. He's never going to be good. Sometimes, you get a goal against because you stay too long, but that was a shot I had to give and it worked."

Cournoyer was 31 when his teammates elected him captain to succeed Henri Richard in 1975. It was an easy choice, Cournoyer was bilingual and charismatic. He was a six-time Cup winner and playoff tough, Cournoyer's average of a goal very 2.2 games remained constant in the regular season and playoff. Cournoyer lacked Beliveau's statesmanlike aura or the incendiary competitiveness of the Richard brothers but was readily accessible and displayed an obvious delight in playing.

"Yvan was a little more outgoing than Jean or Henri was," remembered Peter Mahovlich, "but in the way that mattered they were all the same. That sign in the dressing room about passing the torch on to somebody else, that's the way Yvan was."

He enjoyed three productive seasons with the C, scoring 32, 25 and 24 goals but lingering back pain steadily cut into his play. He underwent major surgery in the spring of 1977, and in 1979 a lumbar disc was removed from his lower back.

The end was rocky. Cournoyer, sure that he was ready to play, was scratched for a road game in Boston and he stayed behind in the Canadiens' dressing room, hammering his hands together and pacing like a caged animal. Then came the final night against Philadelphia, and the end that Cournoyer had hoped to postpone.

Cournoyer didn't know it then, but the day he retired he began a long journey that would return him to the Forum.

"You go out of hockey and when the door closes it seems like you're going to prison," Cournoyer said. "But then you realize it really wasn't."

That realization took time. Athletic gifts, good luck and steadfast devotion to being a Montreal Canadien made it possible for Cournoyer to live his dream but it left no room for life after hockey. While many players dabbled in jobs in the off-season and around hockey, Cournoyer preferred to keep his focus, year-round, on the sport. Change can transform strengths into faults and the very devotion that made him a marvelous player created a huge void when Cournoyer retired.

"It was so very hard for him to accept," said Evelyn Cournoyer, his wife of 13 years. "He went through some very tough times mentally. You wanted to give him suggestions but it really got to the point where you left him alone and let him work his way through it."

The Cournoyers founded a business, Brasserie No 12, in Lachine and it proved to be an acceptable middle ground between business and athletics. The restaurant was patronized heavily by Canadiens, many of whom continued to seek out his counsel. Cournoyer sold the restaurant three years ago and after fruitlessly seeking an assistant's job under then Canadien's coach Jacques Demers, managed to return to the Forum: he was the coach, general manager, owner and even namesake of the Montreal Roadrunners in the Roller Hockey International League.

Still, nothing quite managed to replace the void left by the departure of the Canadiens from Cournoyer's life. "When I built the restaurant it helped to think of something else but I don't think I enjoyed anything more than hockey," Cournoyer said. "Even then, I was missing the adrenaline before the game. There is no place you can have that more than in sport."

The return of Cournoyer to the Canadiens was complete when he was named to the team's coaching staff under old friend Mario Tremblay four games into the 1995–96 season. "Finally," Evelyn said when he told her of the job offer, "we're going to be back where we belong."

Yvan Cournoyer did find one more day in the sun, and it was a glorious one. He skated marvelously, garnered a couple of assists and earned a first-star selection as the veteran Canadiens skated past a squad of NHL old-timers. At game's end, Cournoyer and longtime teammates like Bob Gainey, Steve Shutt and Guy Lafleur circled the ice for a final curtain call as the public address system blared the Queen anthem, "We Are The Champions." " 'This is my last game. This one will be my last game,' he says that all the time," scoffed Evelyn. "He still loves the thrill of playing. With Yvan, hockey was first, not family, not anything else, hockey."

Still, two months after the game, Cournoyer was holding firm. "I wanted my youngest boy, Kurtis, to see me play. He wasn't really old enough before," said Cournoyer. "I gave him my jersey and my stick but absolutely, this was the last time. I was stiff for a week."

CHAPTER 8

BOB GAINEY

CAPTAIN 1981–1989

CHAPTER 8

BOB GAINEY

CAPTAIN 1981–1989

Five days a week for 41 years, George Gainey would turn left out his front yard, walk down Peterborough's Driscoll Terrace, head over the Hunter Street Bridge and finally, right into the Quaker Oats plant. The job waiting for him at "The Quaker" was neither glamorous nor lucrative: he spent almost all of his working life as a shipping and receiving clerk.

George and Anne Gainey raised seven children; Anne tending to the brood, George often moonlighting for a diaper service. All seven of the Gainey kids were raised in the shadow of the plant and the life their father earned for them there. Three of the children became teachers. The others found futures as a dairy farmer, a Carmelite nun, a hockey player and a nurse. The hockey world knows the fifth child, Robert, as Bob Gainey, and the path to understanding one of the Canadiens' most admired leaders inevitably leads back to those thousands of miles walked in five-minute increments between home and the Quaker.

George Gainey's parents owned the house in Peterborough in which he and then his children grew up. He began working at the Quaker in his mid-teens, enlisted in the services in 1943, at the age of 26, and drove a personnel carrier with the Hastings and Prince Edward Battalions in Sicily and Italy before participating in the liberation of Holland. He lost friends in the war, but aside from a cut lip incurred during a Luftwaffe bombing raid, made it home unscathed. Like many men who witnessed intense fighting, Gainey doesn't enjoy talking about it and his family had to press him to gain even the most cursory of details about his life as a soldier.

Anne Crowley worked in the box office of the Regent Theatre and she met George at a dance before the war. A courtship ensued but they did not marry until 1948, two years after his return home. They knew they were in love before George enlisted but held off on marriage to ensure they both felt the same way upon his return. "You didn't want to rush into anything after he was gone for so long," said Anne. "After a person comes back, they need a bit of time."

"I said I guess I'd better have her for a wife," remembers George, tongue planted firmly in cheek. "I told her and she came along."

George never strayed from the Quaker or Peterborough and in those 41 years his wage ranged from 30 cents an hour to $9 upon retirement in 1980.

It has been, he agrees, an ordinary life, rich with work and struggle, celebrated with family. "It has been about as close to average as you can get," says Gainey, now 81, and hampered by a lung ailment. "Working at the Quaker during the week, picnicking and playing with the kids on the weekend. We didn't have a lot, but we had a lot of fun."

"His dad did all the things that good people do," said Red Wasson, a family friend who coached Bob Gainey in minor hockey. "He raised a fine son and Bob carried the sort of character he learned from him into hockey. He'll be a carbon copy of his father which I think is a great compliment."

"His dad is really quiet but very strong, mentally and physically," said Peterborough *Examiner* managing editor Ed Arnold, an old friend of both men. "Bob is like his father in the quietness and class. Without having social class, he's a class person."

Indeed, the greatest commonality between the men is the stature they enjoy in the eyes of their peers, George in Peterborough, Bob all over the NHL. "The only thing I can compare the regard in which hockey people hold Bob Gainey is the esteem baseball people have for Joe DiMaggio," said *Dallas Morning News* hockey columnist Terry Egan. "You won't find anybody willing to say anything bad about Bob Gainey. There just isn't anybody out there."

In 16 seasons patrolling the left wing of the Montreal Canadiens, Gainey did more than score his share of pivotal goals and take on the opposition's most gifted players. He executed the game's minutiae with such relentless brilliance, he elevated the role of hockey footsoldier to a new strata. Along the way, Gainey captained the Canadiens for nine seasons and 569 games. Only Jean Beliveau captained the Canadiens for more games, wearing the C for 679 regular season games.

Gainey was exceptionally talented, but he used his gifts to become the workingperson's superstar, the player who shone not just through his abilities but through his character. He showed up for work every day, regardless of circumstances, and quietly excelled at making everyone else better. There is nothing new in this; George Gainey did it, as did Anne and countless other parents in countless other households. Usually there is no fame in this kind of a life but there is honor, and when you speak of what George and Bob Gainey share, you speak of more than their appearance and their quiet manner. You speak of that common honor.

That said, Bob Gainey has a very mortal patience span and a highly developed pragmatism that would make him a formidable adversary. It isn't that he's not a real person, he's just a very decent one, and Gainey has gained enormous public sympathy and private admiration for the way he dealt with the death from cancer of his wife, Cathy, in the summer of 1995 and the subsequent reverberations her death brought to his family.

A mention of Gainey's off-ice persona prompts a thoughtful nod from longtime teammate Ken Dryden. "Bob handles things the way Bob handles things," Dryden said. "Whether it's as a player, off the ice during that time, or off the ice now, he's a strong, solid, dependable, decent guy. That's the way he'll always be."

In the celebrations that marked the closing of the Montreal Forum, the sounds of 16,000 condolences and whispered encouragements came in the guise of thunderous, emotive ovations whenever Gainey was introduced and the admiration for him extends from his family outwards.

"My brother is talented, and the talent he has happens to be one that is respected and honored in this country," said Maureen Newby, "but I guess that the most wonderful things I have seen in my brother came with Cathy's illness. The way he looked after his wife was amazing. The service and the goodness and the faithfulness right to the end. He treated her like gold."

It is that faithfulness and decency Wasson remembers in describing how Gainey rented a limousine to take Wasson and Ed Rowe, the manager of Gainey's church league team, to his Hockey Hall of Fame induction. He installed them in the second row and introduced them proudly to Philadelphia Flyers' owner Ed Snyder and Dallas Stars' president Norm Green at the reception. "He didn't have to do that, I mean it was his night and we were two guys from Peterborough," remembered Wasson. "But you don't forget actions like that."

Growing up in Peterborough, Gainey said over soup, two nights after the Forum finale, mostly meant not having to try to be someone you weren't. "The environment that I grew up in would have a big effect on many of the ways I would think later on," he said. "If you're running a business selling cars or working in a local factory, you're rubbing elbows with somebody who knows you and your family and your family's family."

In conversation, there is a reserve about Gainey, apparent in the way he stares straight ahead when listening to a question and the pause he imposes before answering. It is an intensity he displayed even as a boy. "He hardly spoke. He was very, very quiet," remembered his sister Maureen. "He would come into the house and sit down and he wouldn't say anything, but there was still that presence."

Gainey remembers his childhood as secure but unexceptional. "It was just an Irish-Catholic middle-class family. My father always worked, my mother was always at home," recalled Gainey. "Four sisters and two brothers. Pretty typical, really."

The Gaineys are Roman Catholic and proud of it. When Gainey was 6, his parents noticed a limp. A local doctor said the problem originated in his hip and there was no guarantee he would walk normally. "The doctor said it could go away on its own or it could be debilitating but I remember at the time feeling he might have been preparing us for the worst," said Anne. "A neighbor heard about the problem and suggested we make a novena (prayer and devotions for nine consecutive days) to St. Jude." The Gaineys prayed and made a request to the local convent, the Sisters of the Precious Blood, for their prayers and the limp quickly disappeared.

"None of us think that it went away on its own," Maureen said. "When you pray you don't always get what you asked for, but you've got to have faith," Anne said. "That's what we've always believed."

Gainey's family had always called him Robert, but around his tenth birthday, they started fielding phone calls for someone named Bob. Even at that age, Gainey had set about defining his identity. "I think it was his way of sort of being independent, of beginning to break away from the family," said Anne Gainey.

"Once I started to play hockey and I was on several teams, Robert seemed to be a more crisp, formal kind of name and Bob was more of a sporty athletic kind of name," Gainey said. "It got changed more by the people around me than by me, but I suppose there's a time in your life where nobody likes their name, so it was an easy change."

By his early teens, Gainey's remarkable skating speed and instinct for the game were evident. So was his tendency to miss the net on the three or four breakaways he earned a game.

"The skills he showed then weren't unlike the skills he showed in the NHL," remembered Red Wasson. "He just got better at them. He was very coachable. If we said, 'Look, this other guy has got speed and he will use it to go wide,' we'd put Bob on him. Other kids don't have the discipline, but he recognized you have to follow a system, even in midget."

Gainey possessed a discipline rare in adults, let alone teenagers, that usually won over his passion during a game. Once, in the final of a heated series against another Peterborough team, Wasson ordered his players to abstain from fighting. The opposition sent its toughest player after Gainey, who took a hail of blows but refused to hit back. "Gainey followed our instructions but it was a sad time from my point of view," remembered Wasson. "He didn't get beat up badly, but he came back to the bench and said to me: 'Don't ever ask me to do that again.' I never did."

Gainey graduated to the Ontario Hockey League's Peterborough Petes and fell under the tutelage of future NHL coach Roger Neilson who at the time was moonlighting from his job as a high school teacher. Neilson saw a team blessed with only limited talent and asked each player to commit to the club in front of teammates.

"We started right at the bottom of the league and changed players and scratched and clawed our way through until we were a much better team at the end of the year," remembered Gainey. "Eventually, we won the OHL and went to the Memorial Cup round-robin tournament in Ottawa."

That playoff run, in which the Petes lost to the Cornwall Royals of the Quebec League in the national final, was a seminal one for Gainey. "I don't know if it was my first concept of team or not," remembered Gainey. " But, I enjoyed that type of loyalty among teammates. It's something that drags you through when things aren't as good as they should be or could be and for me, it was a very rewarding year."

Using a draft choice they had acquired from St. Louis, the Canadiens drafted Gainey in the first round of the 1973 draft. The move to use their first-round draft on a player who had always struggled to score didn't seem quite so shocking for the Canadiens, who in Yvan Cournoyer, Jacques Lemaire and Frank Mahovlich boasted three of the league's top ten scorers the year before. Still, there were questions raised in Montreal and Peterborough. "When he was drafted, we thought 'Heavens above, where will he go there?'" remembered George. "He was a real worker, but he could hardly put the puck into the net."

Gainey was too shy to say anything usable for the media at the draft and his agent, Bob Woolf, subbed for him with the press. That fall, he packed his skates in a car his friend Jack Scriver and another pal had rented and headed for downtown Montreal and the Canadiens check-in. The trio arrived on Friday, the day before the check-in and having no idea what to do in Montreal, went to an Expos game and sat through bone-chilling September cold.

"The next day, when we finally left him at the hotel, he forgot his skates in the car," remembered Scriver. "We had to shout for him to come back and get them and I remember the way he looked as we were leaving. It was almost like he was saying, 'Come on guys, don't leave me here.'"

Gainey scored just three goals in his rookie season of 1973–1974 but in his second campaign he garnered 17. He would hit double figures for the next dozen seasons, never scoring fewer than 12 or more than 23. His first Stanley Cup win came in 1976, his third season with the club, as the Canadiens began a string of four consecutive Cups with a sweep of Philadelphia in the final.

Gainey's ascendancy to the elite level of the NHL coincided with that of the team. Gainey won four straight Frank Selke awards, given to the best defensive forward, from 1978 on, and would have won more but for the fact that his second and third seasons predated the award. If Guy Lafleur, Cournoyer and the big-three defense of Larry Robinson, Guy Lapointe and Serge Savard were the focal point of the team's incendiary firepower, Gainey was the linchpin of the defensive game and it was largely his presence that lifted those editions of the Canadiens from a solid Stanley Cup winner to one of the best teams of all time. "It was a team that won," said former Canadiens' grinder Doug Risebrough, "on scoring and timely defense and Bob was central to that."

"I can't think of anybody on our team who means more to us than Gainey," insisted Serge Savard during the glory years. "A few guys, like Robinson, Lafleur and Lapointe, mean as much. But they're not more important than Gainey."

Coached by Scotty Bowman, the Canadiens led the league in goals against for all four of their Stanley Cup seasons. By comparison, the Stanley Cup winners from 1990–95 finished ninth, 18th, 18th, 14th, third and third in goals against. The Canadiens were also first in goals scored in three of those four championship years, and the proof of that club's place in hockey history is established with the fact that the 1978 Canadiens were the last NHL team to finish first in goals for and against.

In the sixth game of the 1977 semi-final, Gainey scored both goals in a 2–1 win that eliminated the threatening

Islanders from the playoffs. In 1979, he garnered the Conn Smythe Trophy as playoff MVP. The Canadiens vanquished the New York Rangers and Gainey scored the winning goal in Game Two, the tying goal to force overtime in Game Four and Stanley Cup clinching goal in Game Five.

In his wonderful book, *The Game*, Dryden described Gainey as a steward of the game, a player who became far more valuable to his offense-laden team as a 12-goal defensive forward than as a defensively indifferent 30-goal man. Gainey, like all great stars, understood the game's rhythms and had the talent necessary to tap and change them. But Gainey's gift was rarer still; he could stride onto the ice with the Canadiens reeling and leave with the club solidly back in control. Usually, he hadn't even garnered a shot on goal but only the score would remain unaltered when Gainey returned to the bench.

Gainey dominated because he was willing to do more than just perform the drudgery necessary to be a solid defensive player. "I've got good analytical skills, I know other players and other skills," Gainey said. "It wasn't difficult for me to analyze who we were playing against, what their weak points were, what their strong points were, how I could disturb it, how I could become a problem to what they wanted to do."

Most NHLers have a rudimentary understanding of the player they are assigned to cover. Gainey considered it his job to know the strengths and weaknesses of every opposing player. He would play differently against the Maple Leafs' Lanny McDonald than he would against Mike Bossy of the Islanders, not because they were widely dissimilar players but because there was a wide gap in the talent that surrounded them.

"For example, I think in Mike Bossy's case, you had a double-edged sword in that Denis Potvin played behind him," Gainey said. "You had to roll the dice and decide who could do the most damage. That made a big difference. Had Michael Bossy had a slouch behind him at the point, he would have had more difficulty scoring goals than he had."

A superb blend of physical skills allowed Gainey to implement his game. At 6'2" and 200 pounds, Gainey was strong enough to physically handle virtually any powerful forward and fast enough to keep pace with the league's speedier players. Watching Gainey stride into the maelstrom of a game and neutralize an opponent made observers believe he could stick his arm into the spinning tub of a washing machine and pull out exactly the shirt he wanted. "I had the skills to carry it out," he said, with the deliberate precision of a scout dissecting an opponent's game. "I was a great skater. I had size, balance, strength. I knew what I wanted to do, and for a certain period of the 16 years that I played, I could do what I wanted to do."

Former teammate Peter Mahovlich, now a scout for the Edmonton Oilers, said Gainey's physical and instinctual gifts made him a prototype. "Maybe players before him didn't have the speed he had or the size. In the game, there's always a little bit of a change somewhere along the line. Players get a little bigger, faster, and he was one of the players in front of that."

He was also extraordinarily durable. In 1979, when he won the Conn Smythe, he played with a dozen stitches in his forehead and a deep skate cut on his right leg that kept opening and closing. "This guy played with injuries, separated shoulders, things like that," remembered Guy Lafleur. "He was just such a great leader for us." Bob Gainey's playing career was a superb confluence of ability, grit, and the lucky timing common to champions: he was the best defensive player on one of the best teams in history.

"He was a player who brought attention to that role which was otherwise the most invisible role on the ice," said Dryden. "Bob made people understand how important that role was and it took a player of his ability who was at the right place at the right time to do it. Had he played on a lesser team, he would have been invisible even though he played as well as he did. When you're on a team as good as Montreal, a team that is vulnerable in so few ways, the thing you worry about is what the best guys on the other teams can do. Bob came to be front and center in that case. That was the hope that the other team felt, and when you lose that sense of hope, then the rest is awfully hard."

Canadiens' coach Scotty Bowman understood that unlike most players, Gainey didn't have to reconfigure his game to suit the team's demands for defense. The extra ice-time inherent in that allowed Gainey to develop his scoring touch and develop into a big-game goalscorer.

"Bob came up as a defensive player but he developed into a good two-way player because of the role he was put in," remembered Bowman. "He didn't have the offensive responsibilities. He was a strong player; he didn't get a lot of penalties but he played hard-nosed hockey."

In fact, Gainey was a revelation for Bowman, a player humble enough to be unconcerned with statistics but gifted enough to be able to dominate a game in any area of the ice. Immensely coachable, intensely competitive and alert to the game's patterns, Gainey, unlike high-voltage prodigies such as Lafleur, was an asset that required little or no servicing.

"Scotty was able, as he is now, to clear up the confusion," remembers Gainey. "That's what he's done with his own team and he made it very clear what your goals are and what your responsibilities are. If you do it, if you understand it and you accomplish it, there's very little maintenance. If he has to maintain you, there's going to be conflict. I didn't like his maintenance so I tried to stay away from it."

On a team dominated by the presence of Lafleur, the quintessential gifted and mercurial Francophone goalscorer, Gainey existed as a marvelous and equally important counterpoint. Rick Salutin, writing for the *Toronto Star*'s *Today* magazine, said "Gainey is what you would expect to get if you turned Lafleur inside out."

"I guess I can see that," Gainey conceded over soup. "French-English. A little more flamboyant, a little more conservative. A little less dependable, a little more dependable. A little higher top end, a little more consistency. Pretty good balance if you've got the two of them."

The Canadiens played the Soviet Red Army team to a dramatic 3–3 tie on New Year's Eve, 1975, and Gainey's fame quickly spread to both sides of the Atlantic. "Very, very intelligent" player, and "very, very great player," remembered Soviet goaltending great Vladislav Tretiak. "This is very difficult for hockey players. He looked and saw everything all the time. I admired him. He was very important for his team."

On the heels of that famous confrontation, Red Army and National Team coach Victor Tikhonov called Gainey "technically, the best player in the world." Gainey's esteem within the game was cemented.

Only age could defeat that Montreal team. After the 1979 win, the club's fifteenth in 29 years, Dryden and Jacques Lemaire retired. Angry at being shut out of the general manager's job, Scotty Bowman bolted for Buffalo.

Gainey was 27 when, in 1981, the club asked him to assume the captaincy. Not only was he a sterling player, he projected the right image as a family man. "Bob was always putting the effort on the ice, during the practice, during the game," said current Canadiens' general manager Rejean Houle, "but his private life was an example also." Gainey was still in high school when he met Cathy Collins at the Peterborough Arena, where she practiced her figure skating and worked as an usherette. Cathy Gainey, a gregarious and engaging woman, made sure that the club's social circle continued its orbit, welcoming rookies and their wives or girlfriends and making sure no one was left alone on Christmas.

But the team Gainey inherited was nowhere near as talented as the Stanley Cup teams he had already played for. Despite his stewardship, the Canadiens did not return to the final until 1985–86, seven seasons after their last Cup win. That year, the Canadiens rode the goaltending of rookie Patrick Roy to a five-game victory over Calgary.

The fact that he inherited the C during an era dominated first by the New York Islanders and then by the Edmonton Oilers was the only instance of unlucky timing in Gainey's career. That 1986 Cup would be the only championship won under Gainey's captaincy, but wearing the C nevertheless remains his highest achievement in hockey.

"I think I was satisfied that I was able to be the captain on one of the teams that won the Cup because there was a lot of status attached to it, but along with it came the responsibility," Gainey said. "You're supposed to be able to deliver that Cup. Maybe that's part of the reason why 1986 is one of the most joyful Stanley Cups."

Gainey found the role surprisingly political. At first he was too closely associated with the coaching staff, so he discreetly moved to distance himself from the club's management and make himself more available to individual players. Still, when a young Chris Chelios or Petr Svoboda needed to be reminded of his defensive responsibilities, Gainey acted decisively.

"Bobby always walked the great line to being a friend when a player needed it and kicking some players in the ass when they weren't living up to what their obligations were as teammates," Risebrough said. "He had a great ability to reach people and be vulnerable to people. I think sometimes if you're vulnerable to people, you open yourself up, people have a tendency to give of themselves."

"I think that I can usually touch people somehow. I can make them either comfortable if they're not or put them on edge if they're comfortable," Gainey said. "Each team has different kinds of people. You've got your young kids and you've got married people and we had different cultures and maybe not initially, when I became captain, but in the last five or six years I was able to work in all different groups. If I had to, I could go to anyone's house and feel welcome."

In 1989, after series victories over Hartford, Boston and Philadelphia, the Canadiens earned Gainey one more trip to the Stanley Cup finals but the Flames prevailed in six games to hand Gainey his only series loss in the Stanley Cup final.

Gainey, then 35, retired after that playoff. He accrued five Stanley Cups, 239 regular season goals and 501 points. In 182 playoff games he recorded 25 goals and 73 points.

Upon retirement, Gainey looked for a spot within hockey that would satisfy his desire to remain in the game while furnishing more time for his family, and he stunned observers by taking a job with a club team in the south of France. A spot as player-coach for Epinal of the French Second Division meant everything from recruiting players to overseeing and maintaining the ice. Gainey loved it.

"I didn't think going to France was much of a risk, but it was a little bit off-the-wall," remembered Gainey. "I didn't envision myself leaving Montreal but I didn't know what I was going to do if I stayed there. I knew that if I stayed in Montreal I wanted my children to be able to deal in both languages to a good depth. I had visited Europe and I thought it would be a pretty good thing to do."

It was a difficult but memorable year for the children as well as for Cathy, who missed her family in Peterborough. Still, the Gaineys' door remained as wide open for visitors as it had been when Bob captained the Canadiens.

Because of the attributes he displayed as a player, Gainey was widely tabbed as a natural coach but the Canadiens were comfortable with Pat Burns, so Gainey looked elsewhere. The obvious choice was the Minnesota North Stars, who were left without a coach when Pierre Page moved to accept a bench job with the Quebec Nordiques.

Gainey returned to the NHL after one season in Europe to coach the North Stars. "We were looking for someone who had won at the National Hockey League level, who knew the dedication and effort it takes to win," said Stars' general manager Bobby Clarke. "For me, the decision to ask Bob to become coach was easy, because I felt there was nobody better qualified." Gainey would coach the Stars to the Stanley Cup final that year but two months into his job, he picked up the telephone to hear the panic-stricken voice of his then six-year-old daughter Colleen. "Momma's asleep on the bathroom floor," she said, "and I can't wake her up."

Gainey phoned a neighbor who went to the house and helped Cathy regain consciousness. She told her neighbor she had the flu, but a few months later doctors told her she had a brain tumor, the same affliction that had killed her brother and father.

Surgery and radiation treatments seemed to beat the cancer back but an operation was also required, in an area of the brain where her senses, emotions and learning capabilities were stored. Slowly she reclaimed the ability to speak and for a while, her prognosis seemed good. "Let's go, get your uniform and get ready," she shouted one morning to her children as they prepared for school. "Suddenly," she told Ed Arnold, "Laura [her 10-year-old-daughter] came up to me, and she hugged me and said 'Mommy, you're back.' I asked her what she meant. She meant, your voice is back."

Anna Gainey was 13, Stephen, 12, Laura, ten and Colleen six that year. One night Cathy woke up with one child in bed beside her and the others on mattresses around her bed. "Stephen was my knight in shining armor, the man of the house," she told Arnold. "Anna was the doctor, making sure everything was there, my pills and everything else. Laura and Colleen were my spirits. They would cheer me up and keep me happy."

In the summer of 1994, Cathy became ill again and her condition deteriorated steadily. Through it all, Gainey continued to coach and act as the team's general manager, a position he inherited when Clarke left for a job with the Florida Panthers in the spring of 1992. Making the situation even more difficult was an emotional move by the franchise from Minnesota to Dallas in 1993.

"All through that sickness, he was unbelievable with her," remembered Arnold. "She was strong. She refused to die for years and I think it was because of their love."

Cathy Gainey died June 23, 1995, in Peterborough. She was 35. "They didn't want sympathy," Doug Armstrong, the Stars' assistant to the GM said at the time. "Bob and Cathy worried more about other people. They never came across as feeling that their problems were any greater than any of our problems. That's a hell of a quality."

Arnold remembered Gainey summoning him to the house to visit Cathy. "She could barely remember me, and she died a few days later. It wasn't until later that I realized, that's why he wanted me to see her."

Deepening the family's grief was the fact that Laura began to break away during the latter stages of her mother's illness. She began dressing shabbily, her marks slumped and even her body language suggested that she was using drugs.

"What she was doing was burying feelings of anger and depression," Gainey told the *Montreal Gazette*'s Red Fisher. "Anger over her mother's illness. Isolation. Abandonment. The kids, I think, take something like what happened to Cathy as being deserted."

After a hideous scene in which Gainey pulled his daughter out of a neighbor's house where he thought she was using drugs, Gainey took her to a clinic in Dallas. She stayed for less than two months, often using smuggled drugs. In her first weekend home from the clinic, Laura and a girlfriend got into their school and smeared the walls with graffiti. They smashed a photocopier, did $10,000 in damage and left enough evidence to get caught.

The next day, Gainey took Laura to a long-term treatment center in Topeka, Kansas, that treats people for a host of disorders including drug abuse. "She didn't want to go and . . . you don't want to take your kid, and well . . . drop her off some place in the middle of nowhere," Gainey told Fisher. "But it had to be done." Laura was admitted in January of 1995 and she came home nine months later, drug free.

Colleen, now 11, was in a clinic for a month last summer after a bout of depression. As he finishes up his meal with a coffee, Gainey is taciturn about the condition of his children. The ovations in Montreal, while touching, reminded him of his decision to go public with Laura's problems in the hope that other parents would recognize some of the warning signs in their children. "I'm really not comfortable discussing this in great detail," Gainey said, "I don't want people to think that I'm going to the well on this again. For a teenager, Laura is doing OK," he says. "Colleen is doing much better, she is over her depression and she's very active. They still have some therapy."

Midway through the 1995–96 season, Gainey became convinced he had lost the attention of his players and promoted Ken Hitchcock from the International League's Michigan K-Wings to coach the Stars. The move paid no real benefits as Dallas finished last in the Central Division and out of the playoffs, but Gainey has no regrets. "They're being better handled than the way I was handling them earlier in the year," Gainey said. "It's not because I'm a bad coach. If I wasn't coaching well, it was a combination of a little bit of burnout by me between my job and my personal life and the same thing that gets everybody in the NHL, the longevity factor without comparable success to go with it."

His new position means less travel and more time with his children. Stephen is apprenticing in the family business: he just completed his rookie season with the Western League's Kamloops Blazers.

Although Gainey misses Canada, he signed a three-year contract extension that will keep him in Dallas until the year 2000. For Gainey, it's finally time to try to get back to a normal life, to find in the frenetic world of the NHL what another man found in the walk to the Quaker: a sense of place, of duty, of purpose.

"I don't think we've moved completely away from the passing of my wife but it's going to be a year soon," said Robert Gainey of Peterborough. "I think once we go out the other side of that, we'll be all right. Mostly, I'm looking forward to moving on, to moving ahead."

CHAPTER 9

PIERRE TURGEON

CAPTAIN 1995–Present

CHAPTER 9

PIERRE TURGEON

CAPTAIN 1995–Present

As a technician bore away the torch, Pierre Turgeon, surrounded by reporters in the bowels of the Montreal Forum, insisted ghosts could indeed change address. Moments before, Turgeon had accepted the flaming torch, symbolic of the leadership of the Montreal Canadiens from former captain Guy Carbonneau and skated it around the ice. The crowd sang along in a chorus of "Auld Lang Syne" before Turgeon led his teammates off the ice to cap the closing ceremonies for the venerable building.

Now, the flush of excitement still evident in his youthful face, Turgeon was saying all the right things. The essence of the Forum will not be lost, he told the journalists, with the desertion of the arena for the uptown swank of the Molson Centre. "We have the same team, the same organization," Turgeon said. "We'll bring it over there."

Throughout the game that preceded the ceremony and the perfectly choreographed nostalgia that followed, Turgeon had been the quintessential captain. He scored a goal and added an assist, earning first-star status in a 4–1 triumph over the Dallas Stars and drew cheers whenever he touched the puck. Turgeon's play left his coach beaming. "You could see Pierre was psyched for this game," Canadiens' coach Mario Tremblay said. "To lose the last game played at the Montreal Forum would have been unthinkable. He told me, 'Don't worry, Coach, I'm going to have a great game.' And he did."

All week, Turgeon handled the rush of media with uniform grace. When his moment came to usher the franchise into the future, he beamed as brightly as the torch he bore. Turgeon was, in so many ways, perfectly cast as the 22nd captain of the Montreal Canadiens. Married, with three children, he is an unabashed family man. Turgeon is so handsome, veteran hockey writers have joked that he is too unmarked to be a hockey player, let alone a captain. His mother tongue is French but he is fluently bilingual, so he can easily speak with the English media and, unlike his predecessor Mike Keane, understand the nuances of the French press.

Despite the potentially corrosive effects of a contract worth almost $5 million Canadian, Turgeon remains, in demeanor and approach, true to the small-town roots he shares with Jean Beliveau, Toe Blake and Yvan Cournoyer. He looks the people he speaks to in the eye, not out of technique but out of genuine interest. While there is nothing awkward about him, neither is there a residue of polish. Pierre Turgeon, like Bob Gainey and Beliveau, radiates decency; not social graces but grace. "As far as class goes among members of the Montreal Canadiens," *Journal de Montreal* columnist Bertrand Raymond said, "Pierre Turgeon is the cream of the crop."

On the ice, there seems no limit to what Pierre Turgeon can

do. He has scored 30 goals seven times in his NHL career and twice topped the century mark in points. At 27, he is only now entering his physical prime. A playing style based entirely upon finesse has spared him serious injury to the key components of a hockey player's body: back, wrists and knees.

Turgeon has been gifted with tremendous vision of the ice and the refined sense of anticipation only allotted to the game's real offensive stars. Turgeon's passing touch is in the top 10 percent of the league; he can fit the puck into the narrowest margin. He has a very good shot and can work well in close to the net or from the perimeter.

Compared to the other elements of his game, his skating is poor, but Turgeon is, in fact, a slightly better than average NHL skater. "I think he's a much better skater than people think," said linemate Mark Recchi. "He can fly pretty good and when his skating is on, that's when he is at his best." At 6'1" and about 200 pounds, Turgeon is small enough to seem elusive when confronted by bulky defensemen and big enough to generally hold his own.

"Skill-wise, he has everything," said Calgary Flames' director of pro scouting Nick Polano. "He's got size, skills, ability. He anticipates well, he has good vision and as for his speed, he may not be that fast but he gets there on time. There is no question that he should be better."

Better as in a superstar. Despite his salary, despite his position, Pierre Turgeon is not a superstar. He is instead a top-drawer offensive player and had rankings of NHL centers been performed during his career, Turgeon would probably have finished between fifth and tenth virtually every season. The explanations are mostly physical: he lacks the skating and reach of Mario Lemieux or the strength of a Mark Messier. Nor has Turgeon, as those others have, inherited a sterling supporting cast that could both elevate his play and, at times, distract the opposition's checkers. Pierre Turgeon is not a good enough player to turn an inferior team into a Stanley Cup contender. He has the ability and the desire to be a force on a dominating team, but he is not a dominating solitary force. For Turgeon, the explanation lies in circumstance. He has never accepted mediocrity, but he does accept who he is and what he has done and there are precedents for his position: Joe Sakic in his early years in Quebec, Mario Lemieux in his first Pittsburgh seasons and Wayne Gretzky in his last years with Los Angeles. Players burdened with heavy expectations and surrounded by mediocrity do not win. And while the circumstances are forgotten quickly, the failures never are.

For his critics in Buffalo, New York and Montreal, Turgeon's explanations have never been enough. The tension between Pierre Turgeon's ability to accept himself and the inability of those around him to accept what he has done is the story of his past, present and future in the NHL.

And so, 41 days after he carried the torch, Turgeon could not be trusted to carry the play. Whenever he touched the puck in the final moments of the third game of the Canadiens' first-round loss to New York, he was booed by the Molson Centre crowd. Turgeon's apparently lacklustre post-season performance and the Canadiens' six-game swoon in the first round to the New York Rangers prompted journalists and open-line sports show callers to hold a summer-long rehash of Turgeon's value as captain.

Turgeon said the booing and the criticism of his abilities as captain are unfair but easily ignored. "You don't like the booing, nobody likes it, that's for sure," Turgeon said during a driving tour of his hometown of Rouyn-Noranda in early June. "But this is the way it is in Montreal. I can take the pressure and I can do something about it. I can go back there and do something down the line because I am capable of doing it."

His performance in this year's post-season is as good a place as any to try to explain the gap between Turgeon's play and other people's expectations. Turgeon's statistics and the variables surrounding the Canadiens, 1996 first-round swoon refute the theory that Turgeon endured what was, for him, a typical post-season bust. His career points per game and goals per game ratio for regular-season and playoff games are virtually identical; he does not stop scoring in the post-season.

The explanation for Turgeon's perceived lack of production—he had two goals and six points in six games—can instead be largely traced to the team's tactics against New York and some profound weaknesses in the Canadiens' lineup. Rookie coach Mario Tremblay, along with general manager Rejean Houle, knew the best way to shut down the Rangers was to attack their big line of Mark Messier, Adam Graves and Pat Verbeek. The Canadiens, however, did not match up well. Turgeon was neither fast nor physical enough to contain Messier. Houle was never able to land another accomplished defensive center after he included Mike Keane in the Patrick Roy deal, so the job fell to Vincent Damphousse, a career left-winger whose strong skating at least afforded him a chance to keep up with Messier. While not a defensive star, Damphousse, Tremblay hoped, had enough offensive ability to keep the Rangers star on the defensive.

The plan was explained to Turgeon in a private meeting before the series. "The first two games Rejean Houle and

Mario Tremblay said they wanted me to just make sure things were OK defensively," Turgeon said. "I said 'Well, you want me to play that way, I'll play that way.' " The strategy worked to perfection . . . for a while. Damphousse scored twice, including the winner in the opener, and added another pair of goals in Game Two as the Canadiens escaped New York with a 2–0 series lead. Desperate for offense, Rangers coach Colin Campbell kept sending Messier over the boards and when the Canadiens countered with Damphousse, Turgeon saw his ice time cut dramatically.

New York vs second unit featured two premium defensive players in Jari Kurri and Nicklas Sundstrom, as well as the dangerous Luc Robitaille. That line and the Turgeon unit (right-winger Mark Recchi and an assortment of left-wingers) battled to a stalemate with neither side able to break through for a goal. Since Damphousse had outplayed Messier, the Canadiens seemed in the driver's seat and the game plan was exonerated.

Scouts assigned to the series were surprised at how well Turgeon handled his defensive responsibilities but, despite the 2–0 lead, the Montreal media was vexed by Turgeon's lack of offensive production. What no one noticed was that while Turgeon was invisible offensively, he was playing his role to a tee. "I didn't really do anything the first two games; the papers and the fans started getting on that," Turgeon said. "But my coach and the GM were happy."

The Canadiens had hoped their power play would give Turgeon his chance to rack up some points, but there was a major flaw in that game plan. The loss of defenseman Vladimir Malakhov to injury left the Canadiens' power play unit without an experienced point man. The Rangers' penalty killing consisted of collapsing on Turgeon near the New York net and choking off any opportunities he might create. The Montreal power play produced just three goals and converted power play opportunities at a piddling rate of 9.6 percent.

Things began to unravel for the Canadiens in Game Three. Damphousse began to show signs of flagging and the Canadiens could not contain the Rangers' captain. Messier assisted on two first-period goals, both by Adam Graves. The Canadiens countered by boosting Turgeon's ice time and while he mustered three shots, Rangers goalie Mike Richter was outstanding and New York prevailed 2–1.

Turgeon said he had difficulty finding the offensive instincts that he shelved in Games One and Two. "You know how hockey is. You get confidence on one, two or three goals and you go," he said.

Messier and Graves continued to overpower Montreal's defenders. In Game Four, the two combined for three goals and Turgeon's ice time was again boosted. Turgeon scored but the Canadiens lost 4–3.

The series was now racing wildly away from the Canadiens and if there is legitimate criticism to be made of Turgeon's performance, it is in Game Five. Turgeon mustered three shots but the Canadiens were soundly outplayed, outshot 42–27 and fell 3–2 .

Turgeon was the Canadiens' best player in Game Six with a goal and a pair of assists, but the Rangers routed Canadiens' goalie Jocelyn Thibault with four goals in the first 11 minutes. New York, deeper and substantially more talented than Montreal, buried the Canadiens with a 5–3 win.

On balance, Turgeon had enjoyed a mediocre playoff. Had he been able to muster more offense late in the series, the Canadiens might have extended the series. But the New York victory was really built on factors that had little to do with Turgeon. Messier wore down Damphousse and the Canadiens' inability to counter with another first-rate defensive center was a fatal shortcoming. The Rangers' superiority in depth and special teams was pronounced; Messier's linemate Adam Graves scored six times in the series including five times with the man advantage. The Rangers' power play unit clicked on one in four occasions; they outscored Montreal's power play 8–3. The Canadiens' veteran offensive players, Recchi and in particular Andrei Kovalenko, were ineffective. New York goalie Mike Richter outplayed his Montreal counterpart Jocelyn Thibault and the Canadiens' defense turned in an undistinguished series.

Clearly, the series did not turn on Turgeon's perceived lack of commitment. But when he accepted the torch from Carbonneau, one of eight former captains who passed it along, Turgeon also accepted the comparison between himself and his predecessors. Not only was he expected to carry on their legacy, he would be the first one questioned if the gap between this year's Canadiens and those who had come before proved, as it had against New York, too great. It is part and parcel of being the captain of the Montreal Canadiens, the torch can burn as well as illuminate the man who holds it.

Pierre Turgeon's roundabout path to the Canadiens began at the arena that bore the name of his present general manager. Every Saturday morning, Turgeon would rise at 5:30 a.m. and walk four blocks in the dark to the Rejean Houle Arena. He would arrive there at 5:45 and wait for the arena manager to open the door. League play and practice started at 7 a.m. and Turgeon was allowed to skate for 45 minutes or so on the empty ice before the arena bookings began. He spent much of his day at the rink, looking for teams that were shorthanded at practice and wouldn't mind him sitting in.

"It wasn't like it was work or any kind of sacrifice," Turgeon remembered. "It was something I loved to do. You don't get up at 5:30 in the morning when it's minus 35 and go outside unless you really want to."

Rouyn-Noranda is a small Quebec mining town, an hour or so east of the Ontario border by car and nearly four hours north of North Bay. While the town is best known for its extensive copper mining, the area's secondary industry consists of airlifting hockey players to the Montreal Canadiens. They have included Rejean Houle and Jacques Laperierre, former stars of the Canadiens who still toil in the organization, Houle as general manager, Laperierre as a well-regarded coach of the defensemen. Flyers' defenseman Eric Desjardins and Pierre's older brother Sylvain also played for the Canadiens.

Turgeon grew up on the upper floor of a duplex owned by his uncle. Square and utilitarian, it had a back-alley for a backyard and it is here that Turgeon encountered his first athletic accident. At five, on his first try on his two-wheeler, he careened down a steep grade, veered away from an oncoming car and hit a post. Turgeon suffered a concussion and two black eyes. Twenty years later, Nicole Turgeon rolls her eyes and slaps herself on the cheek at the memory. "We had put training wheels on the bike," she says, drawing in breaths as quickly as she did that summer day. "And he just rolled away."

There is much of Nicole in Pierre, the ready smile and brown-green eyes. Marcel Turgeon is much more quiet than his animated wife, and while the vitality essential to Turgeon's character is reminiscent of his mother, his tendency to keep it behind a placid exterior is all his father. Barely 50 and powerfully built, Marcel is as comfortable with silence as his wife is with conversation. For 18 years he fed his family by working as a lumberjack; now, he works for the city of Rouyn and the physical strength of the man runs through big hands and strong forearms.

The Turgeons were already accustomed to the idea that the NHL was within reach. Sylvain, their only other child, was four years older and he had graduated first to the Quebec League's Hull Olympics and then into the NHL. Sylvain was chosen second overall in 1983 and went on to enjoy a productive 12-year career. "We knew from the beginning Pierre would have to leave for his hockey," Marcel said with a shrug. "We did not concentrate on having our son being a hockey player. We wanted him to be a good person. If he was a good person, everything else would follow."

Pierre was not only a great hockey prospect, he was also a promising baseball player. When he was 12, Turgeon, his team's ace pitcher, led the Rouyn club to a fourth-place finish at the Little League World Series.

The next year, Turgeon was at a school social event when schoolmate Elisabeth St. Jacques asked him to dance. Turgeon said yes and the two began to date. Even at 13, they knew they were in love but Pierre's hockey would soon force him to leave Rouyn. Turgeon accepted an invitation to play hockey for a high school in Montreal, where he could continue his development against better competition. Eight months after they met, the two parted. "We knew it would not work with Pierre leaving," said Elisabeth, "but I know that in the back of both our minds, we thought there was a chance we would get back together."

A year later, Pierre was drafted first overall by the Bisons de Granby in the Quebec Major Junior Hockey League draft. The next summer, Turgeon had a girlfriend from Montreal with him when he stopped by the ice cream shop in which Elisabeth worked. Through a frozen smile, Elisabeth dished out a heaping cone for Pierre and a piddling one for his date. The two reunited for good the summer of 1987, when the 17-year old Turgeon stood in the NHL draft. Elisabeth moved in with Turgeon in his second year in Buffalo.

A petite blonde, Elisabeth, like her husband, had to learn English from scratch when she left Rouyn. She is a full-time supporter and part-time nemesis to her mate. For a joke, she recorded all of Pierre's painfully halting first interviews in English and played them back at a family function, convulsing everyone in the room with laughter.

Turgeon and London Knights' forward Brendan Shanahan were considered the two "can't miss" prospects of the draft. The Sabres had finished last the season before, so choosing between the two fell to Buffalo general manager Gerry Meehan. Turgeon scored 69 goals in 58 games with Granby but it was his play in the post-season, the very element for which Turgeon would later be criticized, that attracted Meehan.

"They were playing in the playoffs in the Quebec League. Their team was down 5–2," Meehan said. "Pierre had not done much up to then, and I had made the trip up to Montreal.

Our Quebec scout, Mike Racicot, loved Pierre Turgeon and he was pacing because his guy wasn't playing well for the boss. In the third period, within a very short period of time, Pierre scored two goals and set up another one and they won the game. I was impressed by his ability to take control of the game and be the difference. That's what I always felt you were looking for, a player willing to take the responsibility of being able to deliver in the crunch. And whenever I saw him, he came up with the big plays."

Meehan took the gamble, but awaiting Turgeon in Buffalo was a spectre he could never shake. In 1970, the only other time they had the first overall choice, the Sabres selected the most dynamic player in franchise history, Gilbert Perreault. From the moment he set foot in Buffalo, Turgeon would be compared to Perreault. There were obvious similarities. Both were centers; both were French and from small Quebec towns, Turgeon from Rouyn, Perreault from Victoriaville. Both were number one overall choices who had assembled impressive numbers in junior.

But it was an odious comparison. Turgeon's game was totally dissimilar from that of Perreault, one of the most gifted skaters in the game's history. "Perreault had everything, absolutely everything to score 50 goals and get 120 points a year," said *Buffalo News* hockey writer Jim Kelley. "Perreault was better than Pierre in a lot of ways. Pierre is a very good hockey player but don't expect too much of the kid. People have always expected 50 goals and 120 points and I don't know that he is good enough to do it game in and game out." "I kept on telling people that I can't replace Gilbert Perreault," Turgeon said. "I can't skate like him. My main thing was just to do the best Pierre Turgeon could do."

And so, a month after his 18th birthday, Pierre Turgeon, who had never played a moment of premier level pro hockey, was dropped into the best league in the world. He was told not to worry about justifying his club's selection or his $100,000 salary while living in a foreign country and learning a new language. Eager to shine, Turgeon scored 23 points in his first 30 NHL games but soon ran out of gas.

Kelley remembered sitting beside Turgeon during flights in his rookie year and noticing how the rookie stared, transfixed, out the aeroplane window when the plane began its descent into the lights of a big city. To Turgeon, the cities below were like different planets.

"I couldn't speak a word of English, not even 'Hi, how are you doing?' nothing," Turgeon remembered. "I lived with a family who only spoke English. They helped me a lot but it was tough."

"People do not understand how difficult it is to break into the league as an 18-year-old who can't speak English," remembered Rick Vaive, an NHL veteran who was finishing up his career in Buffalo during Turgeon's first few years with the Sabres. "It might be easier for a guy who is outgoing but for a guy like Pierre, a very private person who couldn't speak much English, it was a very difficult situation."

Considering the adjustments he had to make, Turgeon's 14-goal rookie season was satisfactory and the post-season ended on a high: Turgeon scored four times and added three assists as the Sabres lost to Boston in six games, and in doing so, served notice of future stardom.

"My best Pierre Turgeon story is the way he played against the Boston Bruins in that first playoff," said Clark Gillies, another veteran playing out the string during Turgeon's early years. "He was the star of the series. We got beat 4–2 but he was playing like a full-grown man."

In his second and third seasons, Turgeon upped his goal totals from 34 to 40 and the predictions of superstardom seemed to be coming true. But the Sabres continued as play-off busts: they fell to Boston in five and Montreal in six to drop their fifth and sixth consecutive playoff series. Turgeon scored five goals and recorded 14 points over those 11 playoff games but that was not enough. The Sabres had already made a coaching change, jettisoning Ted Sator for Rick Dudley without any results. The Sabres were now Turgeon's team and if they could not win in the playoffs, the culprit, at least partially, had to be Turgeon.

In 1990–91, Turgeon buckled under the pressure of the expectations and slumped to 32 goals. Questions about his character began in earnest. It was an inquisition that irritated Meehan. "I've often thought the media can be faulted for creating expectations and reputations that aren't really true," Meehan said. "Pierre is a fine person and a fine athlete. If you ask me to balance on the plus side and the minus side, the number of times he exhilarated plus the times he disap-pointed me, the exhilarations would far outnumber the disappointments."

Turgeon was, in fact, ineffective and discouraged for stretches in Buffalo and if this is a failing, it also reflects the fact that he is human. "Yeah, there were questions about his heart," said Gillies. "But you know, when you're a young guy and the other team knows that the key to beating your team is to stop you, it takes an awful large pair of you-know-whats to fight through it night, after night, after night."

"I would say my fourth year in the NHL, playing with Buffalo, I found it tough," Turgeon said. "I learned a lot from that year. Why? Because that's hockey, that's life. You're trying hard, but sometimes it doesn't go the way you want it to go. You're going to have some great nights, you're going to have some ups and some downs. It won't be the same all the time. They say, how can you appreciate the good times if you haven't seen bad?"

More bad times followed when the Sabres fell again in the first round, this time to Montreal. The team's ownership made another coaching change, replacing Dudley with former Edmonton coach John Muckler. Muckler, whose Edmonton teams were based largely on speed and power and the cockiness those two elements created, inherited an underachieving team led by a player who had none of the virtues he valued. In the playoffs against Montreal, "Guy Carbonneau would punch him in the mouth in the first game," said one Buffalo official, "and Turgeon would disappear for the rest of the series."

Eight games into the 1991–92 season, Meehan traded Turgeon to the New York Islanders in a seven-player deal. The Sabres were in the initial stages of setting up a pitch for a new arena and were looking for a star. One was available in the Islanders' Pat LaFontaine, who had been involved in an ugly contract war in New York, and Turgeon's lustre had been tarnished by defeat. "We wanted LaFontaine as the player to build around," said Muckler. "We wanted a cornerstone. We felt Pat LaFontaine was the cornerstone and cornerstones are expensive. Turgeon had to be part of the deal. That's the reason why we traded him."

Kelley, however, felt Turgeon was taking the blame for the lack of post-season success. "What killed Pierre Turgeon in Buffalo was the fact that he couldn't take the Sabres out of the first round," Kelley said. "I don't think they expected him to deliver the Cup, but they thought he could lead them into the finals, something like that. But neither he nor the team were ready for that. It was an unfair expectation."

Fair or otherwise, Turgeon, Benoit Hogue and Uwe Krupp moved to the Islanders and surrounded by a better talent level, Turgeon scored 38 goals. More importantly, he regained his confidence.

The next season, 1992–93, was the finest year of Turgeon's career. He scored 58 goals and finished with 132 points to lead a resurgent Islanders team. Al Arbour, who had coached earlier editions of the Islanders to four Stanley Cups, inherited a career year from goalie Glenn Healy, a talented and precocious cadre of defensemen led by rookie Darius Kasparaitis, a slate of useful character players and the best set of linemates Turgeon has ever played with, left-winger Derek King and right-winger Steve Thomas.

But Turgeon's dream season came to a crashing halt in the final moments of Game Six of the Islanders' series-clinching first-round victory over Washington. Turgeon had his arms in the air and had just scored the insurance goal in what would be a 5–3 victory when Washington center Dale Hunter smashed him from behind, sending him crashing into the boards. Turgeon suffered a separated right shoulder and was lost to the Islanders for the balance of the next series.

Hunter, long one of the NHL's dirtiest players, claimed not to have known the play had ended. Commissioner Gary

Bettman, along with the rest of the hockey world, didn't believe him and Hunter was suspended for 21 games the following season. While the Islanders would record a stunning seven-game upset of Pittsburgh in the next round, Turgeon, playing hurt, was ineffective in the third-round loss to Montreal.

Aside from a chilly phone call, Hunter and Turgeon have never spoken of the incident. "He called me two days after it happened," Turgeon said. "He apologized and said he hadn't seen me or something. It was only two days after and it was a cold conversation. I said thanks for calling and that was it."

The Hunter hit, described by *The Hockey News* as "The Cheap Shot Heard Round The World," cost Hunter $150,000 in lost salary, but the cost to hockey in New York might have been even higher. "That hit changed hockey history," said New York *Daily News* hockey writer Frank Brown. "Pierre Turgeon had been a dynamic, involved personality. He was becoming the emblem of the Islanders and the club was saying: 'This is our symbol of future greatness to come. This is the offensive superstar we haven't had since Bossy and this is the hope for a bright new arena on Long Island and million-dollar visibility in the marketplace.'

"Everything, changed by one mean-spirited little prick. When Pierre Turgeon got up, he left some piece of himself on the Nassau pond. From the minute he returned, he was hesitant; he was a perimeter guy; he was a guy who was not activating the energy level of his team the way he had been. He didn't have that drive to the front of the net. He never gave you the sense that he was worth a penny of what he was being paid."

Turgeon maintains there were many reasons, other than the hit, for the Islanders' subsequent collapse. Healy was left exposed in the expansion draft after the club acquired Ron Hextall but the move backfired when Hextall was routed in the 1994 playoffs. The club's young defense, particularly defenseman Darius Kasparaitis, took a step back. Turgeon missed 12 games when he was hit by a puck during a pre-game warmup in Toronto, but still managed 38 goals and 94 points. But Gillies, one of the tougher wingers to skate in the NHL, said the Hunter hit scared him and wondered if Brown wasn't right when he claimed Turgeon was permanently spooked by the incident. "It scares you, it would scare the best of us," Gillies said. "That somebody has the ability to do that to you . . . you never know when it's going to happen again."

"The mental damage lingered, as far as everyone could ascertain," Brown said. "We had seen what Turgeon could be, the curve was upward, upward, upward and when he plummeted there was no climb back. There was just a walk along the floor of a canyon. It was not going to get better. He had to go."

Turgeon dismisses the criticism; the incident, he said, did not change his game one iota but circumstance changed the team's level of success. "What he [Brown] said doesn't matter, that doesn't matter at all," Turgeon said. "You know why? The season we had was big for me and big for my linemates. Steve Thomas and Derek King had 40 goals. It was a year, everybody was going in the same direction and the whole team was going well. We had Healy who was giving us good goaltending. Sometimes it's just a big wheel going in the same direction.

"Now, I'll ask you the question, Why didn't the Devils win the Stanley Cup again this year [1996]? The answer is, the year they won [1995], they had a year where the timing and everything else was there . . . the timing, who they played against. They played well. Why didn't they win the year after? Because there were 24, 25 teams who wanted to win more."

In April of 1995, retooling once again and desperate to forge a team with a more blue-collar image, the Islanders sent Turgeon and Vladimir Malakhov to Montreal in return for Kirk Muller, Matthew Schneider and Kirk Maltby.

"I liked where I was and I would have been satisfied even if I didn't come here, but to come to Montreal is to come to another level," Turgeon said. " I don't know if I ever believed I could play for the Montreal Canadiens."

Turgeon scored 11 goals in the 15 final games of the season for the Canadiens, but despite his heroics, the club missed the playoffs. In December 1995, when Patrick Roy demanded and was quickly granted a trade out of Montreal and took Keane with him, Houle and Tremblay named Turgeon captain.

Many fans and members of the media wondered if the C would not sit better on Damphousse. "The big issue was the opening of the new Molson Centre," said Bertrand Raymond. "The Canadiens wanted someone who projected a family image. Damphousse was a bachelor and there had been problems in behavior with some of the captains who had been bachelors. The captain probably had to be French and he had to be a big name. That meant Pierre Turgeon."

Raymond believes Turgeon hasn't risen to the league elite because he tried too hard. "The Islanders found that the more they asked of Pierre Turgeon, the lower his production became and I think the same thing is happening here."

Canadiens general manager Rejean Houle concedes the C is in recognition of the person Pierre Turgeon is and the player he might still become. "We appreciate what he is giving but we know that he can do more and we feel by giving him the C he will get there," Houle said. " He will find through the years, himself, as an individual, he's got a lot of resources and he'll be able to give more to the team, not just as an individual scoring but as an example to the other players."

His 38-goal, 96-point 1995–96 season was, to many, a typical Pierre Turgeon year: two goals shy of 40, four points shy of 100 and a poor playoff to boot. "The only area he doesn't score highly in every night," said Nick Polano, speaking for most everyone in the league, "is drive."

And so the debate over Pierre Turgeon's character rages on, as it will until he retires or finds himself on a good enough team to win the scoring title or even the Stanley Cup. Until then, Turgeon says, he will not change. "I don't know if I can grow on the ice because of the C on the jersey. What I did last year or the year before, that's the player I am."

WHERE ARE THEY NOW?

Newsy Lalonde, 1917–1921: A brilliant Hall-of-Famer who played for five teams, Lalonde scored 441 goals in 365 games. He died, November 21, 1971, in Montreal at the age of 83.

Sprague Cleghorn, 1921–25: A robust defenseman and crowd favorite, Cleghorn died at the age of 66 in Montreal.

Bill Coutu, 1925–26: Coutu played 10 years for the Canadiens before being traded to Boston in 1927. In his second season with the Bruins, he slugged an official both on the ice and later in a dressing room and was barred from the NHL for life. He returned to his hometown of Sault Ste. Marie and held an assortment of jobs, including one as a security guard at an old-age home. He died in 1977 at the age of 84.

Sylvio Mantha, 1926–32, 1933–36: A hard-rock Hall of Fame defenseman, Mantha worked as an NHL linesman and AHL referee after his retirement and was a longtime minor hockey coach in Montreal. He died August 7, 1974. He was 71.

Babe Siebert, 1936–39: Siebert, a one-time Hart Trophy winner who played defense and left wing, was 35 when he drowned near St. Joseph, Ontario in 1939.

Walter Buswell, 1939–40: Buswell, was a conservative defenseman who retired in 1940 at the age of 32. He lived to be 84.

Toe Blake, 1940–48: Blake, who died in 1995 at the age of 82, has his name on the Stanley Cup 11 times, eight as a coach and three as a player. Blake, former Canadien Jacques Lemaire and one-time Ranger Frank Boucher are the only players to have scored a Stanley Cup–winning goal and coached a team to a Stanley Cup victory.

Bill Durnan, 1948: Durnan reached the NHL at the age of 28 but he won the Vezina Trophy in six of his seven seasons in Montreal. He died at the age of 65 in Toronto.

Emile Bouchard, 1948–1956: Big Butch, at 76, remains in excellent health. He is the oldest-living Canadiens captain and promises to stay in that role for many years to come.

Maurice Richard, 1956–1960: The great Rocket turned 75 on August 4, 1996.

Doug Harvey, 1960–61: Harvey, who died in December of 1989 at the age of 65, is still regarded by many as the greatest defenseman who ever played.

Jean Beliveau, 1961–71: Jean Beliveau is retired, which is to say he has cut the number of boards of directors on which he sits to four.

Yvan Cournoyer, 1975–79: So far, Yvan Cournoyer has stayed true to his promise of never playing again. His wife, Evelyn, remains skeptical.

Serge Savard, 1979–81: Savard won seven Stanley Cups as a player and two as a general manager. This was not enough to deflect the anger of Canadiens' fans over the trade of stars like John LeClair and Chris Chelios for little return. Savard was fired four games into the 1995–96 season and replaced by Rejean Houle. Savard is part-owner of the Chateau Champlain in downtown Montreal and would not return phone calls requesting an interview for this book.

Bob Gainey, 1981–89: Gainey, 42, signed a contract extension with the Dallas Stars that will see him work for the club into the end of the decade.

Guy Carbonneau and Chris Chelios, 1989–1990: Carbonneau, 36, remains a member of the Dallas Stars. Chelios, 34, won his third Norris Trophy after another outstanding season in Chicago.

Kirk Muller, 1994–95, 1995–96: Disappointed at being traded to a New York team, Muller, who captained the Canadiens' 1993 Cup win, held out from the Islanders for most of the season and was traded to Toronto in January of 1996.

Mike Keane, 1995: Keane was traded along with Patrick Roy to the Colorado Avalanche for Andrei Kovalenko, Jocelyn Thibault and Martin Rucinsky, December 6, 1995.

Pierre Turgeon, 1995: After the first four games of the opening-round series against New York, Pierre Turgeon had one goal, one assist and ten shots. Over the next two games, both losses, Turgeon collected one goal, three assists and eight shots.

INDEX